QUEST FOR SNOWDONIA

QUEST FOR SNOWDONIA

The Historical Landscape

Derek Williams

© Text: Derek Williams

Copyright © by Gwasg Carreg Gwalch 2001.
All rights reserved. No part of ths publication may be reproduced
or transmitted, in any form or by any means, without permission.

ISBN: 0-86381-680-0

Cover design: Sian Pari
Cover photo: Rhodri Clark

First published in 2001 by
Gwasg Carreg Gwalch, 12 Iard yr Orsaf, Llanrwst, Wales LL26 0EH
☏ 01492 642031   ▤ 01492 641502
✆ books@carreg-gwalch.co.uk   Internet: www.carreg-gwalch.co.uk

About the author:
Derek Williams, Head of Geography Bala Grammar School, Hawarden Grammar School, later Saltney High School, B.A. (Hons) Aberystwyth, M.Ed. Bangor; Lecturer in Bangor University (Extra Mural Dept.) 1960-1997.

Cerys
For Cerys with love.

CONTENTS

Preface
1 Ice Age Legacy – Lakes GR700 665 10
2 Stone Age Axes – Llanfairfechan GR690 735 12
3 Neolithic Tomb – Capel Garmon GR818 544 15
4 Chambered Tomb – Maen y Bardd GR740 718 18
5 Standing Stones – Tal-y-fan GR739 736 20
6 Uncovering a Beaker – Bwlch y Gwrhyd GR713 678 22
7 Bronze Age Axes 26
8 Bronze Age – Gold Objects 28
9 Tumuli – Burial Mounds GR829 682 31
10 Bronze Age Shield – Moel Siabod GR705 547 34
11 Iron Age Fort – Pen-y-Gaer GR750 693 36
12 Iron Age Firedog – Capel Garmon GR815 550 39
13 Iron Age Settlement Huts 41
14 Riddle of the Bowl from the Grave GR948 500 44
15 Roman Coins GR815 820 47
16 Roman Milestones GR718 716 and GR677 730 49
17 Roman Baths (Caerhun) GR776 705 54
18 Roman Fort – Bryn-y-Gefeiliau GR745 573 58
19 Early Christian Stones – Penmachno GR790 506 62
20 'Celtic Bell' – Dolwyddelan GR736 522 64
21 Motte and Bailey Castle (Aber) GR656 726 66
22 Aberconwy Abbey (Conwy) GR782 776 69
23 Effigy – Betws-y-Coed GR796 566 72
24 Medieval Castle – Cwm Prysor GR758 369 74
25 Richard II's Ambush Site GR884 786 77
26 Dolwyddelan Castle GR722 523 80
27 Dolbadarn Castle GR585 598 83
28 Foelas Castle GR870 523 86
29 'Levelinus' Stone GR869 522 89
30 Coed-y-Ffynnon – Penmachno GR804 531 91
31 Church – Ysbyty Ifan GR844 489 94
32 Hafotai – Aber GR667 704 97
33 Maredudd ap Ieuan – Dolwyddelan GR742 508 99
34 Plas Iolyn GR881 503 102
35 Giler GR884 499 106
36 Cruck Barn at Hendre Wen GR806 588 109
37 John Ogilby's Maps 112

38 Tai Unnos 115
39 Quakers (Memorial – Celyn Reservoir) GR876 405 118
40 Drovers – Bridge at Tai Hirion GR804 398 120
41 Cae Coch Cottage GR733 715 124
42 Water Mills – 18th Century 128
43 Arennig – Abandoned Quarry Village GR833 393 131
44 Turnpike Trust Road GR721 580 134
45 Cerniogau – Coaching Inn GR905 505 137
46 Stage Coach at Ty'n y Coed GR734 572 141
47 Crossing the Conwy Estuary GR790 780 144
48 Stable Lofts – Frongoch GR903 394 147
49 Trefriw Spa GR778 653 150
50 Chalybeate Well at Ysbyty Ifan GR846 485 153

PREFACE

This book was written in retirement after thirty-five years teaching Geography and Geology in schools in Flintshire and Bangor University extra-mural classes at Mold and Wrexham. It was my good fortune in the early days of my research and field-work that I met Frank Jowett. Frank had made an inspired discovery of a Roman milestone in 1954, which confirmed the route of the Roman road over the bleak pass of Bwlch y Ddeufaen to their major fort at Caernarfon (Segontium). We spent many days at sites all over Eryri and submitted our work independently to the North Wales Weekly News. This book is based on articles that I wrote in the newspaper and in Country Quest.

Some features are referred to under their Welsh names throughout. This is especially true in the cases of rivers and lakes, for the vast majority have only ever been known by their Welsh names. Therefore, the words afon/afonydd (river/rivers) and llyn/llynnoedd (lake/lakes) are the preferred forms. You will come across Cwm and Dyffryn, which mean Valley or Vale, and the word Mynydd means Mountain. Also, although the title of the book is Quest for Snowdonia, to delve deeply into this all-embracing and at the same time, elusive area, the journey is made easier by conducting it in a name that has long resounded from the valleys and mountains, Eryri.

The interior heartland of Eryri is still, fortunately, a natural landscape. The historical landmarks selected in this book are mainly found in the valleys, such as those of Afonydd Llugwy, Lledr, Seiont, Prysor, Tryweryn, and particularly Afon Conwy. Lastly, although much of the area discussed is within the bounds of a National Park, some of the features are on private land or are private residences. It is invariably better to check before trudging over property, than trying to explain one's presence to an irate householder or land owner. In most cases they are knowledgeable people who are justifiably proud of the piece of heritage that is in their custody, and more than happy to share it with people who show genuine interest.

1. ICE AGE CLUES TO SECRETS OF THE DEEP
ICE AGE LEGACY – LAKES (GR 700665)

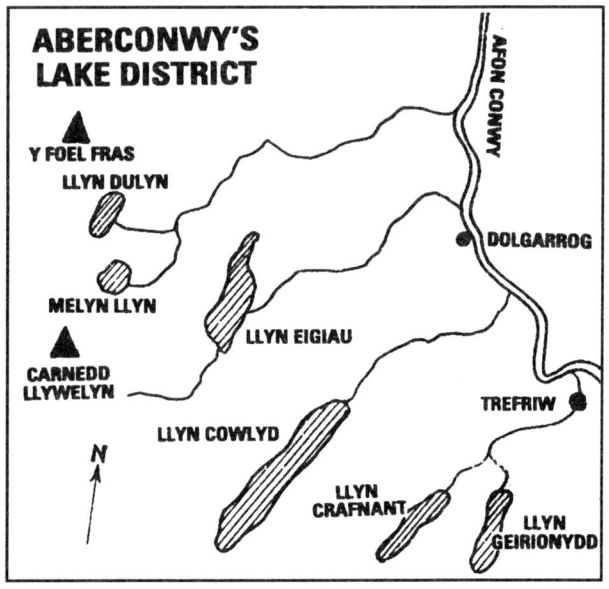

Some of the finest lakes in Eryri lie in the mountain valleys between Carnedd Llywelyn and the Conwy valley between Dolgarrog and Trefriw.

On a sunny day in the clear waters of these mountain lakes, a diver would be able to see the orange life-jacket of the person left behind in the dinghy. At 100 feet (30m) the sun would be visible as a red ball shining on the surface of the lake. At 150 feet (45m) the diver would need artificial light to see in the inky darkness, but he or she could then descend to almost 200 feet (60m) in a number of the high-level lakes in Eryri.

Llyn Dulyn reaches a depth of 189 feet (57.5m), exactly the same depth as Llyn Llydaw at the foot of Snowdon. T.J. Jehu carried out a survey to find the depths of the lakes in 1901. He sounded a number of the lakes and his results, although using only a lead weight, are accepted as being fairly accurate.

He sounded Llyn Llydaw by lowering the plumb-line at a number of regularly-spaced points to find the deepest points. In the late 1960s, sub-aqua diving teams confirmed his measurements and are reported to have noticed holes on the floor of Llyn Llydaw which could have been made by Jehu's plumb-line sixty-five years earlier. If this is correct it indicates that there had been practically no silting up and no disturbance to the lake bottom sediments in these quiet, dark waters.

In the mountains above Dolgarrog there are a fine series of high-level lakes which, together with smaller lakes above Betws-y-coed, form Aberconwy's own 'Lake District'. One of these, Llyn Dulyn, lies in a deep, semi-circular hollow under the slopes of Foel Fras. At 1747 feet (532m) above sea level it is high up and practically surrounded by bare rock and crags, except on the eastern side where a grassy boulder-strewn slope lies near the outlet. Even so the outflowing stream cuts through solid rock and proves that the entire lake exists in an excavated rock basin.

Llyn Dulyn, like its neighbour Melynllyn, lies in a cwm that was occupied and reoccupied for long periods by glaciers. The weight of the ice in the glacier, its forward movement and the boulders, exerted downward pressure and eroded a deep, rock basin in each cwm. At the end of the Ice Age – about ten thousand years ago – the glaciers also left a natural dam of rock waste at the lower end of the rock basin where it melted.

The deepest lake in Eryri is Llyn Cowlyd with a maximum depth of 222 feet (68m) and its underwater contours are shown on the Ordnance Survey map. It occupies a rock-cut basin but there is no semi-circular cwm around it to account for erosion by a local glacier. It is probable that a large glacier streamed eastwards from Carnedd Llywelyn through the low gap into the Cowlyd valley, and was able to cut the deep basin in which the lake now lies.

Llyn Eigiau also has a different pattern, it lies two miles down valley from the high ridge of Pen yr Helgi Ddu. Vast rock crags rise precipitously, from its surface and give an idea of the volume of frost shattered rocks dislodged during the Ice Age in these valleys. A striking feature is the large area of flat land at the head of the lake, once the former bed of the lake.

2. ANCIENT AXE MEN ON THE PRODUCTION LINE
STONE AGE AXES – LLANFAIRFECHAN (GR 690735)

South-west of Penmaenmawr, there are three oval or circular outcrops of rock that were formed when North Wales, from Cadair Idris to Conwy, was subject to regular eruptions of volcanoes – molten lava, ash, 'bombs' and dust particles.

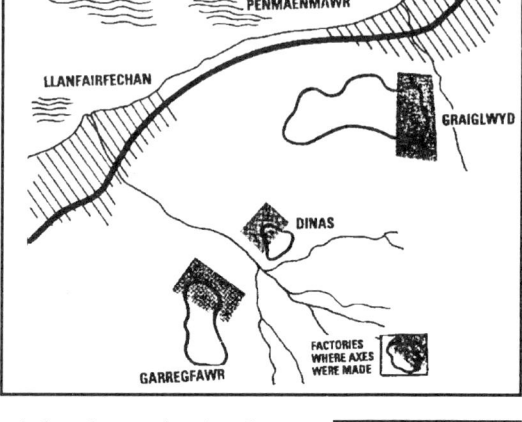

A skectch map showing the axe factory sites on the slopes of the mountain above Penmaenawr

The edges of these volcanic vents are places where the red-hot lava from deep-seated reservoirs beneath the earth's crust cooled so quickly that the rock has only fine crystals. This fine crystalline rock has a black, glassy appearance and splits along saucer-like fractures, so that by chipping the face of the rock, sharp edges separating the fractured areas can be produced.

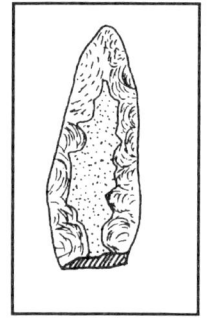

Sketch of a Stone Age axe found at Foel Lwyd

These sharp edges gave early man his first tools, which he could use to cut up animal flesh for food, scrape skins for clothing and, in the form of large axes, cut down trees. The Neolithic or New Stone Age People lived mainly by hunting animals, but needed to fell trees to clear areas for crop growing.

The three weathered outcrops that are found here, formed of augite granophyre, could be used for making primitive stone axes. Unlike flint, these rocks could not be chipped in the hand. Instead, stone age man used flat anvil stones that he placed

Garreg Fawr, Llanfairfechan

horizontally before him as he squatted in the scree. The anvil stones, together with thousands of chips and flakes that are a few feet thick in places, as well as charcoal and burnt earth give a vivid picture of the manufacturing process on the 'factory floor'. Very few finished axes were found here, but the sites yield layers of chips and flakes lying around the flat anvil stones.

They used hard pointed pebbles for hammering the axes to the desired shape. In some cases, the rough-outs had their flaked surfaces cracked by fire. Axes were found in various stages of manufacture, but no polished axes were found in the 'factory' itself.

The earliest finds of these axes were made on the slopes of Graig Lwyd above Penmaenmawr. In the 1920s, working floors were found in the fields above Graig Lwyd farm, below the modern quarry tips. The type of rough-out found there suggested that one person or a small group worked the screes. Dozens of large cores were found, some of them two feet (60cm) long, and are now in the National Museum in Cardiff. Similar axe factories were found on the slopes of Garreg Fawr and

Dinas to the south of Llanfairfechan.

The chance of finding anvil stones, chips, flakes and roughed-out axes are still good in these areas. Search the screes on the north side of Garreg Fawr and Dinas because some may have been lost on their way down river. It is believed that cores, or rough-outs, were taken from the screes to the nearby seashore or steam beds where they would be polished.

The axes were used locally, and many have been found along the North Wales coast from Ynys Môn to Prestatyn. They were also 'exported' to other parts of Britain. Examples have been found in south Wales, the Severn valley, Yorkshire, and the chalk areas around Stonehenge, which was a centre of Neolithic settlement.

Such a wide distribution of stone axes shows that Craig Lwyd axes were able to compete in their day, and we are talking about 4000BC, with the finest flint axes that were found in the chalk beds of southern England. They are similar in shape to the famous flint axes mined at Grimes Graves in Norfolk.

A walk on the northern slopes of Garreg Fawr and Dinas may still perhaps yield an ancient stone-axe left behind, because of some imperfection as a cutting tool, by the first inhabitants to use the volcanic rock of Penmaenmawr.

3. THE SECRET ENTRANCE TO A VAULT OF STONE
NEOLITHIC TOMB – CAPEL GARMON (GR 818544)

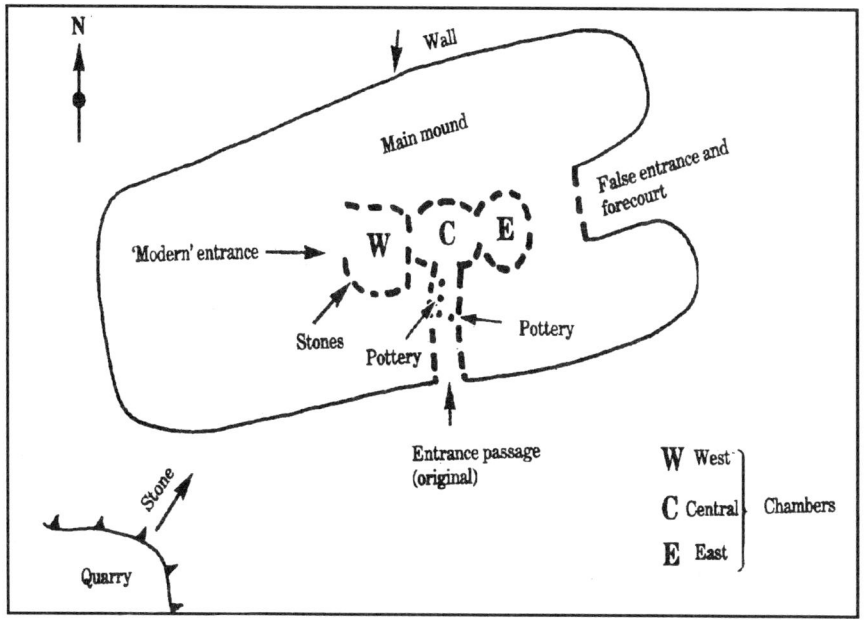

A plan of the chambered tomb at Capel Garmon, showing the false entrance

The chambered tomb south of Capel Garmon is worth a visit for the view alone. On a flat terrace strewn with rock outcrops, at 800 feet (240m), it commands a stunning panoramic view of the mountains of Eryri.

The tomb lies in a field called Cae'r Ogof (field of the cave); the term 'cave' may come from the tomb itself which, although concealed originally under a long mound of stones and earth, was known to have underground chambers. In 1699, it is mentioned as a mound of stones and earth covered by oak and ash trees, with three cromlechs, two of which had broken up. A cromlech is a monument of four or five upright stones supporting a flat capstone. The three cromlechs were parts of a long narrow chamber which can be seen today.

In 1924 the trees were cleared and the site excavated. The stones were reset and the walls, which had been dislodged by tree roots and weathering over the numberless centuries, were consolidated.

What looked like the entrance, with two projecting 'horns' and a forecourt, was found to be a false entrance. It did not lead into the underground chamber and may have been a ruse to protect the tomb from robbers. A ceremony might have been held in the false entrance to accompany a burial in the tomb. Scattered white quartz pebbles were found, perhaps having a magical or religious purpose.

In its original state the whole feature would have been a long, smooth mound blending in with the surrounding fields and small rock outcrops. The sides of the chambers and entrance passage consist of upright stones, probably quarried locally, left in their rough state and embedded in the clay floor. The intervening spaces were filled in with dry-stone blocks. They were built with great skill with nothing more than stone-age tools. The method of wall building kept the tomb clear and access could be made at intervals. In some cases many individual burials have been found, suggesting that these tombs were used for collective burials over a long period.

The main roofing materials were three large flat slabs, corresponding with the three chambers that are visible today. These capstones were of volcanic ash, which outcrops only a few yards to the south-west of the monument. The entrance passage on the south leads directly into the central chamber. Five pieces of red pottery were found in the entrance passage and one of much older black pottery. The red fragments are part of a decorated 'beaker', a type that was introduced by newcomers to the area known as the 'Beaker People' at an early phase of the Bronze Age (about 1800BC).

The black pottery is Neolithic, from about 3,200BC: it is likely that these New Stone Age people built the original monument which was later taken over by the Beaker people, since the two

Capel Garmon cromlech

types of pottery were found in the same place. The pottery is of great value because it gives a reasonably accurate date for the period of when the tomb was in use. Similar burial chambers are found in south-east Wales and in the Cotswolds. The long barrows were probably brought by people from Western France via the Bristol Channel.

The isolation of Capel Garmon from the Cotswold-Severn area may be because it was the work of a group of Neolithic people who travelled overland, attracted by the stone-axe 'factory' at Penmaenmawr.

Other tombs such as Maen-y-bardd, this one being a round tomb, suggest that from about 3,000BC Neolithic farmers began to establish their farms on the hills overlooking the forested Conwy Valley.

4. VOICES FROM THE TOMB
CHAMBERED TOMB – MAEN-Y-BARDD (GR 740718)

Maen-y-bardd near Ro-wen

The impressive burial tomb of Maen-y-bardd lies on the side of the Roman road from Ro-wen to Abergwyngregin. The road itself followed an older track, which goes back to the Bronze Age and even possibly to the New Stone Age (Neolithic) settlers.

This was an important line of communication across the pass of Bwlch y Ddeufaen, between Drum and Tal-y-fan and two large standing stones in the pass confirm its importance as a prehistoric track.

Maen-y-bardd is a cromlech, or burial chamber, with a large capstone resting on four upright pillars, and a few scattered blocks surrounding the base. It remains as a substantial relic to the earliest colonists of the Neolithic period, 4,000 to 3,000BC, who settled in the Conwy valley and its bordering hills.

There are eight such megalithic tombs in the Conwy valley, but these first farmers were not as attracted to this area as others, since they left scores of similar tombs in Ynys Môn and the coastal plains of western Gwynedd.

The stones at Maen-y-bardd are the remains of what was originally a single chamber of a tomb covered over by a circular mound of earth and stones. It was probably entered by a passage from the side of the mound or cairn, which has vanished completely apart from a few blocks in the grass around the upright pillars. The area around has been farmed since prehistoric times, and the original cairn may have been a useful source of stone for building retaining walls and, later, field boundaries.

These megalithic tombs are therefore sometimes reduced to their largest stones, known as megaliths, which were too large to be removed. Their survival in the present landscape, after 5,000-6,000 years is a great tribute to their construction. Their building was a communal effort to provide a 'resting place' for members of the group, rather than a tomb for an important chief. They represented the community's attitude, and as its only public monuments, were the focal points of major social and religious ceremonies in the life of the people. These burial chambers sometimes have the remains of as many as fifty individuals secured inside passages or galleries leading to a central chamber.

Such cromlechs and chambered tombs are found along the west coast of Wales from Ynys Môn to Penfro *(Pembroke)*. The megalithic builders are thought to have originated in the Mediterranean basin because the people found in the tombs are of short, mediterranean build, and similar tombs have been found in Crete, Minorca and mainland Spain. These people moved along the Atlantic coast, bringing their way of life and cromlechs to Brittany, Cornwall, Ireland and Wales.

Stone monuments such as Maen-y-bardd have, because of the size of their stones and method of construction, survived despite the weather, grave robbers and the cultivation of the land around them. They are, however, best regarded as the legacy of a great religious idea which, like Christianity and Islam, had its roots in the Middle East and then spread westwards.

5. "MILESTONES" ON THE MOUNTAIN TRACKS
STANDING STONES – TAL-Y-FAN (GR 739736)

A strong sense of prehistory survives in Tal-y-fan, the mountain range rising dramatically 2,000 feet (610m) above Conwy. The long, spectacular ridge, with its

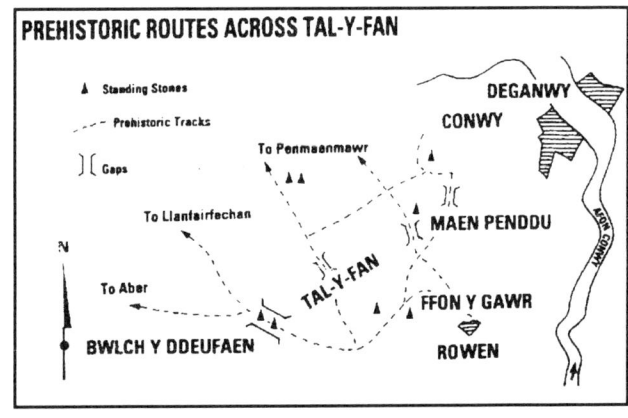

adjoining and higher summits of Drosgl and Drum, attracted early inhabitants because of its hill pasture, its stone outcrops for building, and its high-level springs. Evidence of early settlers at about 1300 feet (400m) is abundant, and include cromlechs, stone circles and hilltop forts.

Hill-walkers today are curious about the isolated standing stones with old-established names. The most prominent of these ancient menhirs are shown on the Ordnance Survey map.

The nearby pass of Bwlch y Ddeufaen is itself named after two stone pillars near the head of the pass. Another well-known stone is Maen Pen-ddu at the meeting place of footpaths on the northern flank of Tal-y-fan. The strangest-looking pillar is Ffon-y-cawr, (the Giant's Walking Stick) over 7 feet (2m) high and leaning at a steep angle. This may be the oldest of all the stones and may have inspired a sense of awe in prehistoric peoples, and in the Roman soldiers who left it undisturbed only yards from their road from Caerhun to Abergwyngregin.

These menhirs were put up by prehistoric man, and often occur in such groups. Other areas where they occur are south-eastern Ynys Môn and the ancient trackway in the hills to the east of Harlech. They are not easy to date and their exact purpose is not certain. Some clues have been provided by their distribution, and excavation of the nearby area sometimes yields a few finds. At Bedd Branwen in Ynys Môn, a standing stone was incorporated in a Bronze Age tomb (barrow), itself raised as a burial mound about 1400BC. In Meirionnydd, the standing stones lie in lines that marked a trackway used by Bronze Age traders and smiths. Some of their axes and weapons have been found in concealed hoards along the ancient tracks.

Maen Penddu near Llangelynnin

The pillars of Tal-y-fan have a striking pattern relating to prehistoric routes. These go back to Neolithic times and were used by axe-traders from the 'factories' around Penmaenmawr. These tracks, originally worn by the footsteps of man and animals, are still used by hill-walkers today.

The paths follow the valleys and cross the ridges where easy gaps occur, and this is where the standing stones are found. They often lie at junctions where hill-tracks converge, as at Maen Pen-ddu. Stones that are found where there is evidence of Bronze Age settlement may be connected to the ceremonial activities centred on the stone circles. Charcoal and pottery found near the stones have been radio-carbon dated to 1400BC (Middle Bronze Age), just before the climate of the hills deteriorated. There is no pattern to the shape or size of the stones, and they include stones that are rectangular, rounded, pointed or sometimes squat. The smallest are two feet (60cm) high, ranging to stones over 12 feet (3.6m) high, which form a striking element in the landscape today.

6. UNCOVERING A RARE BEAKER
UNCOVERING A BEAKER – BWLCH Y GWRHYD
(GR 713678)

Perhaps as you are reading this, there is a coffee beaker in front of you. It is probably about 3½ inches (8.8cm) high with a diameter of over 3 inches (7.6cm). Bangor Museum has part of a small beaker like this, which has an interesting story to tell.

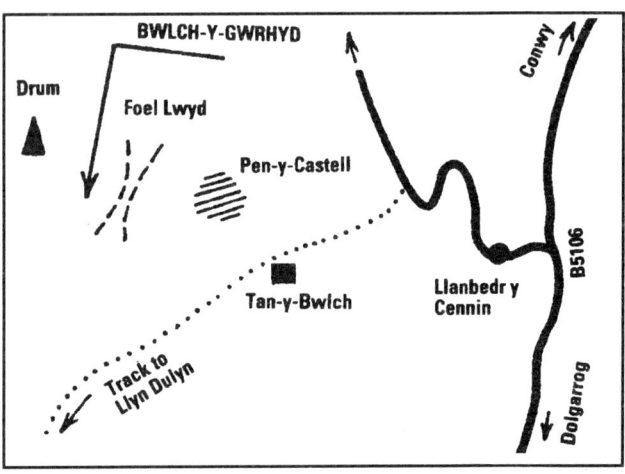

Location map for an important find

We know what it was like because it was perfectly preserved although it had been lying under layers of peat for 4000 years. In Lowe's book The Heart of North Wales, published in 1912, there is a photograph of the beaker which shows it intact and described as 'Urn, Bwlch y Gwrhyd'. Bwlch y Gwrhyd is a bleak pass at 2,300 feet (700m), lying under the summit of Drum. in Eryri.

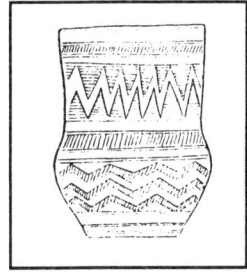

Chevron design beaker
(courtesy of R.CA.H.M)

At some time after 1913 the beaker was broken, and only half of it has survived. However photographs and drawings show its scale and decoration with great accuracy. It was 3½ inches (8.8cm) high and 3.7 inches (9cm) in diameter across the top, where it was widest. It was made of dark brown clay, including well-crushed grit. It is recognised as a long-necked beaker classified as 'A' type and made about 2000BC at the end of the Neolithic period (New Stone Age), at the dawn of the Bronze Age. The decoration consisted of finely notched horizontal lines under the rim, with panels of chevrons and ladders separated by horizontal notches so that the whole beaker was covered. These designs indicate that it was of special importance and was totally different from the contemporary coarse black pottery used by the Neolithic people for storing and cooking. Numerous such beakers from around 2000BC have been discovered, when copper and tin were incorporated to make bronze implements and thus replaced stone axes and flints. Such beakers provide a means of defining the change over from Neolithic stone users to the use of metal. They also marked the change from communal burial in large chambered tombs to burial of individuals in stone-lined graves sunk in the ground.

The distribution map of beakers in Western Europe shows this great change originating in Spain and spreading to Italy, France, Germany and the Netherlands. This 'invasion' or mass-migration of beaker-makers spread to Eastern England and then westwards into Wales as far west as Ynys Môn and Llŷn. It is possible that these 'Beaker Folk' swept across flint-using Neolithic Europe, crushing all resistance. However these beakers may have been introduced more gradually by refugees or by trade.

Archaeologists now take the view that Beaker Culture was adopted and adapted by local societies who were open to new ideas at the beginning of the second millennium BC. They blended the new metal-using technology and religious ideas with their own cultural traditions so that the Neolithic period merged gradually into the new Bronze Age. Powerful chiefs needed to show their rank through objects that were included in the burial site – a beaker, a bronze dagger, jet beads and even cloth; in some waterlogged areas of eastern Yorkshire, massive oak coffins have been found. Over the years the body has left little trace – perhaps a skull and one or two leg bones – so that the beaker is the main find when the grave is opened.

The Bwlch-y-Gwrhyd beaker was buried high up in the mountains at a time when the climate was warmer and drier than it is today, and peat had not yet developed. Later, as the climate got cooler and wetter, peat and moss developed on the wet slopes and by today six feet of peat has grown over these Bronze Age burial mounds.

The circumstances of the discovery of the beaker are worth recording. About 1890 William Jones who lived in Tan-y-bwlch farm found the beaker when he was cutting peat for fuel. The exact find-spot was not recorded at the time and Lowe, writing in 1913, claims that the cairn where it was found was 'on the slope running down from Drum to Pen-y-gaer known as Bwlch y Gwrhyd at a height of about 1800 feet' (550m). This is well above the normal level at which beakers have been found, and Lowe's estimate of its height and location needs to be examined.

A strong clue to the find-spot can be found in the Enclosure Award of 1858 for Caerhun parish. Following the enclosing of open common lands on the mountain, the farmers were no longer able to cut their vital winter supplies of peat in the traditional areas near their farms. The 1858 Award stated that a tract of land known on their map as Block 4, consisting of 54 acres (22 hectares), was to be used exclusively to supply peat for the poor and the upland farmers of Caerhun parish. This block of land is to the south-east of Drum and well below Bwlch y Gwrhyd. It lies between Afon Garreg Wen and Afon Ddu, and there is good footpath access from the farms to the south. A footpath runs directly from Tan-y-bwlch farm, where William Jones lived, which was less than two miles (3.2km) away. He was acknowledged as the finder of the beaker. The exact spot is likely to remain unknown because the tumulus or cairn itself was probably removed by peat cutting. It is however clear that Block 4 is where the beaker was buried four thousand years ago.

The peat-cutting area is south-east facing, rising from 1500 feet (457m) to over 1800 feet (550m) in the north-western corner so that it agrees with the height claimed by Lowe to be the level at which the beaker was found. An easy footpath runs from Tan-y-bwlch to Block 4 and continues across the block to 1800 feet (550m) and then continues westwards to the pass below the high summit of Garnedd Uchaf. Clearly Block 4 is where William Jones in 1890 broke into the stone-lined cist and disturbed the beaker grave. If Lowe is correct in his assessment of the height of the find-spot, it can then be confidently located in the north-western corner of Block 4 at SH713678.

Peat has invaded the hills especially since the Bronze Age, so that burial sites such as that at Bwlch-y-Gwrhyd are still (thankfully) buried beneath the peat, and await discovery.

Roger Whyte of Cae Coch, high up on Bwlch y Ddeufaen, drew my attention to the Census Returns for Tan-y-bwlch and the Enclosure Map of 1858. Information from these sources finally resolved the issue of where the beaker was found. It was not found on Bwlch-y-Gwrhyd and should probably be renamed the 'Garreg Wen Beaker' after the named place nearest to where it was found. Bwlch y Gwrhyd itself is half a mile (800m) to the north and, at 2,500 feet (760m), was well above the limit of peat cutting in the 19th century. Peat cutting was a hard and laborious job and it is surprising that they took the trouble to handle the fragile pot with such care and report it. Other Bronze Age objects, such as the fine bronze shield found in a peat bog on Moel Siabod, can be seen in the British Museum. The whereabouts of its find however, and perhaps associated treasures, have been completely lost.

7. AXE MAKERS SHAPED THE BRONZE AGE
BRONZE AGE AXES

The commonest weapons and tools in the Bronze Age were axes, and the earliest examples were simple, flat tools. They appeared in the early Bronze Age, soon after 2,000BC, and were highly efficient compared to the Graig Lwyd stone axes, which they replaced.

The bronze flat axe, made of copper with some tin, was hafted onto a right-angled stick to hold the axe, and then bound with string. One found by a tree-cutter at Trefriw, in 1926, was 8 inches (22cm) long, and had been hammered into shape. The cutting edge was damaged. A similar flat axe was found at Dolwyddelan in 1880 when workmen were digging the foundations for a house at Tan-y-bwlch. The blade was smaller, being only five inches (12.7cm) long, and had a very sharp crescent-shaped cutting edge, still in good condition. Another was found at Conwy, on the western slope of the rock on which the castle is built, but this one was pitted and corroded.

As time passed the axe-smiths discovered that by hammering or casting upwards, they could form flanges along the sides of the heads that gripped the shaft more firmly. A hoard of seven flanged axes were found in May 1935, about 100 yards (90m) from the summit of Moelfre Uchaf, overlooking Betws-yn-rhos. Mr E. Roberts of Abergele was walking over the hill and, when near the summit (1298ft/396m), saw a piece of metal sticking out of the surface in a patch of ground that was not covered by heather. He scratched the surrounding area and unearthed a hoard of axes at about 9 inches (23cm) below the surface.

The bronze axes were identified with deep flanges and had been made from the same mould. Most were in excellent condition and the finest specimen was put on display at the National Museum at Cardiff. The axes were 6 inches (15cm) long and had been secretly hoarded in a shallow pit at a point near the summit which the smith would have been able to locate later.

These high moors were attractive to Bronze Age man, and were possibly travelled by smiths or traders, carrying their goods for sale. Finding seven axes together at one spot suggests that they were deliberately placed in the ground to be collected later. Such hoards are common in north Wales, and were sometimes hidden under a protective stone. Axes in particular would have been an important source of wealth and power at this time. Perhaps the smith feared that he might be waylaid and his valuable implements stolen. Some hoards consist of scrap metal, cakes of copper, and smiths' tools, rather than finished axes, thus indicating that the smiths travelled around with their materials.

In the Middle Bronze Age (about 1400BC and later) the palstave appeared. This was an axe with a stop-ridge between the flanges to prevent the haft driving down too far and splitting. In the Late Bronze Age (750BC onwards) the technology had improved sufficiently for the smiths to produce a socketed axe in which the haft was stuck into a socket so that there was no danger of splitting the handle in use. A fine example of a socketed axe was found on Conwy Mountain towards the summit of Penmaenbach. One of the largest collections of axes, consisting of fifty palstaves, was found 'within a field in Gloddaeth' as mentioned in a letter written by Richard Mostyn dated 14th January, 1694.

The smiths were busy producing a wide range of products including leaf-shaped swords, sheet-metal of high quality, cauldrons and circular bronze shields. The finest example of a shield was found in a peat bog on Moel Siabod. The exact find-spot is not known but the likeliest place would be on the south side overlooking Dolwyddelan where peat-bogs occur around Llyn-y-foel. The area around the Conwy valley has yielded more than its fair share of bronze axes and weapons, and there are probably many more still to be found when the ground is disturbed by planting trees, ploughing and cutting foundations for roads and buildings.

8. GOLD OF THE CRAFTSMEN FROM BEYOND THE SEAS
BRONZE AGE – GOLD OBJECTS

A Bronze Age Tumulus

A mark of wealth and status, gold objects appeared in North Wales during the Middle and Late Bronze Age (1500-750BC). The gold was from Ireland, found in the gravel river beds beneath the Wicklow mountains, which can be seen on a clear day from the mountains of Eryri.

Trade with Ireland brought gold to harbours at Tywyn, Harlech, Llŷn and Ynys Môn. The gold was made up by Irish smiths who introduced sheet metal work of the finest quality in the Middle and Late Bronze Age. The results have been unearthed during the past one hundred and sixty years in parts of north Wales where Bronze Age people lived. In the Conwy area the best finds were two gold ear-rings found in 1898 along with a Bronze Age axe and an awl beneath a large loose rock near Pigeon's Cave, on the eastern side of Y Gogarth (the Great Orme), just below Marine Drive.

The cave is unlikely to be a burial site, so the find was probably a personal hoard hidden for collection at a later date. The ear-rings would grip the lobes of a lady's ears but, strangely, do not form an exact pair. They were slightly different in diameter and thickness, and one was decorated. A similar find at Gaerwen in Ynys Môn, may have been part of the 'export' trade using the same routes from Ireland.

Another trade route entered north Wales near Tywyn, Meirionnydd and followed y Ffordd Ddu across the northern slopes of Cadair Idris. Here in 1823 a gold rope-like necklace, called a torc, was found in a heather bank on the surface. A smaller torc was found near Harlech. A gold 'lunula', which was a moon-shaped collar, was found in a meadow near Bryncir in Llŷn. Over ninety examples of these finely-decorated gold collars have been found in Ireland.

The largest prehistoric gold object found in western Europe was at Mold in 1833. A Bronze Age burial mound excavated whilst levelling a field contained a stone-lined cist, or grave, which had unfortunately collapsed and crushed human bones and a skull, three hundred amber beads and a sheet of gold. The gold object was the front and back of a ceremonial cape that covered the chest and shoulders of the corpse. The sheet was ornamented with bosses, ribs and arcs beaten into the gold by skilled craftsmen. The amber beads may have been an associated necklace, and indicated ceremonial use. It has been dated to the latter half of the Middle Bronze Age.

A recent find was made in the limestone hills near Eryrys, to the west of Mold. A geology student first noticed a Bronze Age socketed axe wedged in a narrow crevice in the limestone and partly-covered by soil. The hollow axe contained two gold bracelets, which had been twisted and folded and pushed inside the socket of the axe, to hide them.

There was also a small gold ingot, made from melted-down

ornaments. The hoard was deliberately hidden and was declared Treasure Trove at a Coroner's Court. The axes head itself was one of the finest specimen found in Wales and could be closely dated to about 800BC.

These objects found by chance in North Wales show high craftsmanship in the Middle and Late Bronze Age. They were associated with burial or deliberately hidden as a hoard.

Only a few hundred years later, in the Iron Age, gold objects became rare, suggesting that gold mining in Ireland was beginning to fail.

9. BURIAL MOUND HID CLUE TO URN PEOPLE
TUMULI – BURIAL MOUNDS (GR 829682)

There are superb panoramic views of Eryri's mountains from almost any point on the B5113 road as it runs from Pentrefoelas to Colwyn Bay, high above Dyffryn Conwy (valley). The finest viewpoint is probably the lay-by above Soflan, on the Nebo road (B5113) which shows a panorama of Eryri mountain peaks. Another fine viewpoint is the summit of Mwdwleithin about 2½ miles (4km) south-east of Eglwysbach. This long moorland ridge has three large

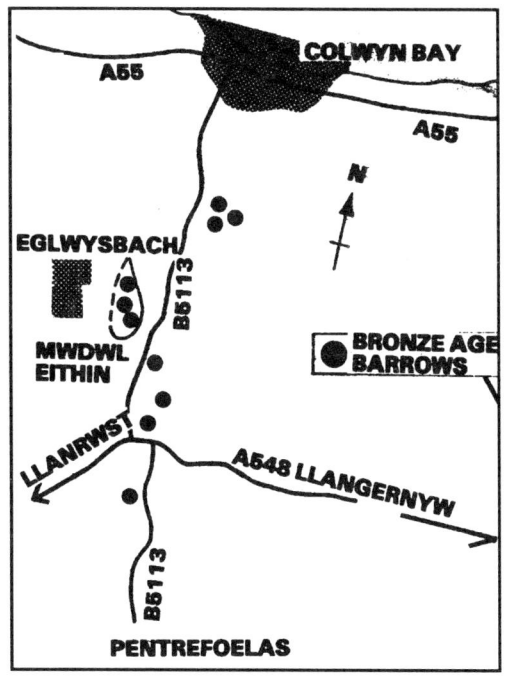

A map showing Bronze age barrows in the Conwy Valley

mounds or barrows which have been notable landmarks on the skyline since they were built in the middle phase of the Bronze Age. No actual settlements of Bronze Age people have been found in this area so we have to rely on their burial mounds for evidence of their funeral customs, their pottery, and items of stone and bronze.

In the Middle Bronze Age (1400-1000BC), the practice of cremation had replaced burial, and this led to the development of pottery urns specially made to contain ash and fragments of bones. These urns were then placed beneath mounds called barrows. A large number of these lie on either side of the B5113, and are shown by the word 'tumulus' on the Ordnance Survey maps.

One of the most striking is a large, oval-shaped mound on the summit of Mwdwleithin. Until the discovery of this barrow in the early years of this century, Mwdwleithin had remained an undisturbed, heather-covered moorland. The barrow was excavated in 1911-12 by the eminent archaeologist, Dr Willoughby Gardener, and it was found that it consisted of white and black layers of clay and peaty soil. These were laid so neatly that it is thought that the turf and the underlying clays were cut in blocks by wooden spades, carried in baskets and put carefully in place. No ditch was found, so it is probable that the material was dug some distance away.

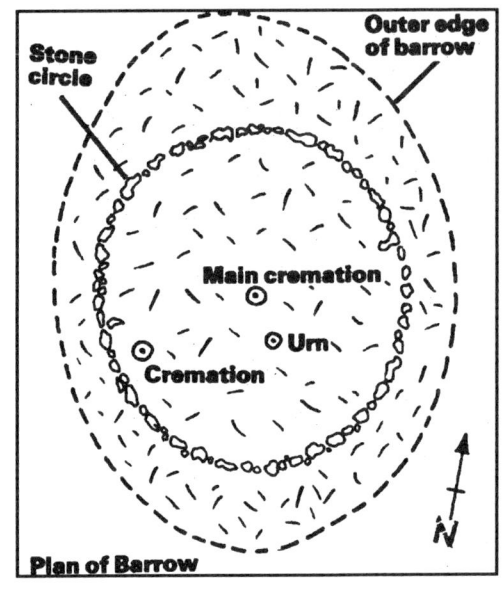

A sketch of the Mwdwleithin barrow, showing the location of the burial stones and urn

The mound was smoothed off about 9 feet (2.7m) above the original flat-topped surface, and the ground underneath was undisturbed and stony, which may explain why local materials were not used. The excavation took five workmen six days, and the main surprise was the find of a stone circle of large stones and boulders lying inside the mound, 15 feet (4.6m) from the edge. The largest stone was 4 feet (1.2m) high, some were upright, and smaller stones in between completed a rough wall.

The stone circle was important in the ritual of cremation and its construction was a vital activity. In the exact centre of the stone circle they found a small heap of ash and bone that belonged to an important local inhabitant, and the reason why the circle and its covering barrow were made. They also found within the circle two later, secondary cremations, the ash and bone fragments from one of which were found in an urn placed upside down under some flat stones.

Over the years these slabs had crushed the urn so that, in 1911-12, only fragments were recovered, but enough to make a reconstruction of the urn. It was similar to the one shown in the diagram – about 12 inches high (30.5cm) and 10 inches (28cm) across. The main decoration were horizontal lines crossed by zig-zags on the overhanging rim, which were impressed in the soft clay by cords of twisted fibre. The surface of the pot was plain, and probably smoothed by hand. There is evidence that it was formed of clay that was found in the mound itself, and was therefore made on the spot.

Although fairly thin and fragile, many of these cinerary urns have survived, and a visit to the Grosvenor Museum, Chester, or Bangor Museum of Antiquities, will show fine specimens. They are vivid reminders of the building customs of our Bronze Age ancestors who lived in a slightly warmer and drier climate on our moorlands.

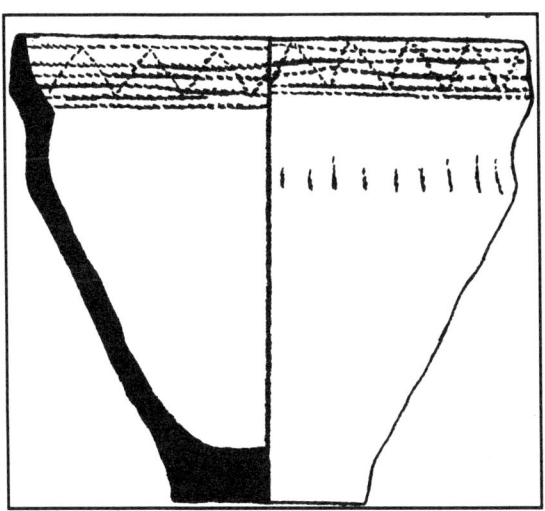

Diagram of cinerary urn Mwdwleithin

10. BRONZE AGE WARRIORS
BRONZE AGE SHIELD – MOEL SIABOD (GR 705547)

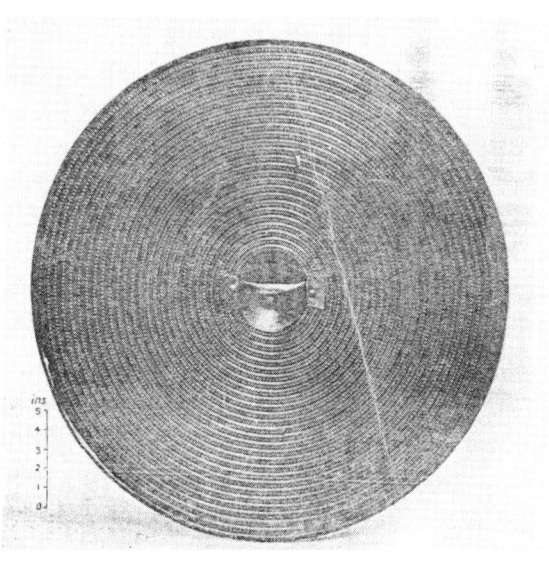

Moel Siabod shield

The recent debate at NATO headquarters in Brussels about the introduction of new weapons is only the latest phase of an ancient, ongoing story. Over three thousand years ago in the Late Bronze Age, the smiths of western Europe were busily producing new weapons that included leaf-shaped swords, socketed axes and shields.

So many finds have been made that it is possible to draw a detailed picture of a Bronze Age warrior with a heavy sword, helmet with cheek pieces, a breast plate, spear and a circular shield. These were the first armoured warriors of 'barbarian' Europe, and can be dated to 1000BC to 500BC. The sword widened to a leaf-shape, and had a heavy blade that was carefully moulded and cast in one piece.

These leaf-shaped swords have been found at Penrhyndeudraeth, Dolwyddelan and also on the high slopes of Carnedd Llywelyn. Bronze working reached a high level of technology with the highest skills of the smiths devoted to weapons, particularly swords and shields. An array of the new weapons began about 1200BC and are found across western Europe from Hungary to Ireland.

Ireland was an important source of copper, and bronze

products were exported. But in north Wales there were also travelling smiths who used local ores from Eryri and Y Gogarth *(the Great Orme)*. No workshops have been found but the furnace was probably a small bowl, and moulds of stone, clay and bronze have been found, including some at Penmachno.

The most interesting find from this period in the area of Dyffryn Conwy is the fine bronze shield found on the slopes of Moel Siabod. The shield was found in 1784 in a peat bog and it is in excellent condition. It is now on display in the British Museum.

The shield has a diameter of 25 inches (51cm) and is circular in shape. It was held by grips made of strips of bronze, rivetted to the back of the shield. The front was highly decorated with twenty-seven concentric circles of small embossed knobs with intervening raised rings. The strength and design are outstanding features of the craftsmanship. A similar shield, although with a damaged edge, was found at Gwern Einion near Llanbedr, Harlech. It was found standing on end, also in a peat bog.

Both shields have a central boss that protects the grip, and were clearly intended for violent use rather than for ceremonial purposes. The coast around Llanbedr is known for finds of Bronze Age materials, and these may be due to the import of copper and bronze from Ireland.

Moel Siabod may have been a trade route across north Wales and its shield may have been lost or hidden in the peat bog from which it was retrieved perfectly preserved. Because the find-spot is not known, no exact date can be given for the shield because no associated dateable objects were found, and the depth of covering in the peat is uncertain. But because it is similar to other shields found in western Europe, it is likely to have been made between 1000-500BC when these sophisticated weapons were abundant.

11. STONE FORT'S 'SECRET WEAPON' REVEALED
IRON AGE FORT – PEN-Y-GAER (GR 750693)

Pointed stones outside Pen-y-Gaer fort

The Iron Age Celtic people had a good eye for hill-tops that afforded them security in an age (about 600BC to the Roman period) when defence was a major concern. At Pen-y-gaer above Llanbedrycennin, they selected a splendid hill with a steep north and east side which today gives spectacular views of Dyffryn Conwy (valley) and the mountains of eastern Eryri.

On the broad, flat summit, they built a high wall, now reduced to five feet, which can best be seen at the main entrance gate. The massive dry stone blocks were partially removed to build boundary field walls when the common land was enclosed two hundred years ago.

Apart from the main stone wall, they also built outer walls of earth and loose stones which they dug from ditches. These can still be clearly traced around the edges of the hill-fort. The

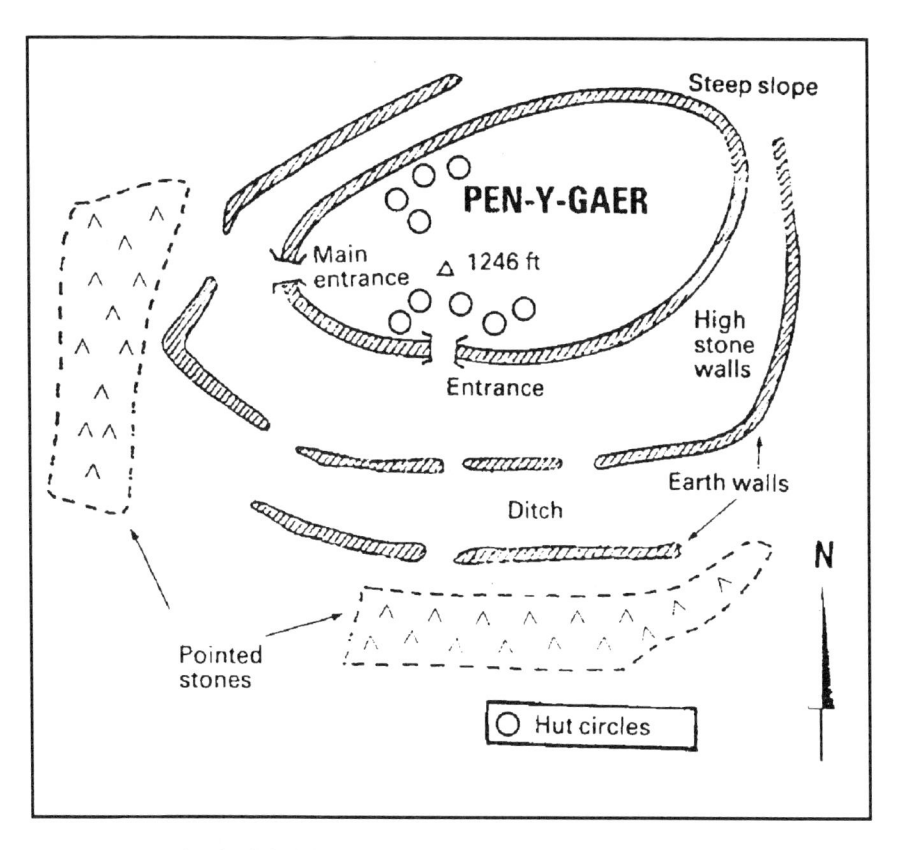

A sketch of the hill fort's lay-out, showing the intricate defences.

western and southern slopes were the easiest side for an attack, so the inhabitants devised a secret weapon. This was noted by the traveller Thomas Pennant in 1775 when he visited the fort and noticed 'two spaces below the ramparts thickly set with sharp-pointed stones set upright in the earth; these were chevaux de frise.'

Two hundred years later than Pennant, and two and a half thousand years after they were first placed there, these sharply-pointed stones can still be clearly seen in two places on the western and southern sides, just below the two main entrances.

The Celtic inhabitants collected suitable pieces of rock (rhyolite and slate) found on the hill top, and then split and trimmed them into pointed spikes. They then cleared the space down to the red-clay floor and set the spikes pointing up with about 18 inches (45cm) of the stone sticking above ground. They were spaced out at 12 inches (30cm) apart and would have been almost impossible to cross. They would have contributed greatly to the security of the residents of Pen-y-gaer.

Over the centuries rain, frost and snow have partly broken up the pointed stones. In many cases the stones have fallen and been incorporated into the soil. Even so, these early 'mine-fields' of stone spikes can still be clearly seen and still make a formidable line of defence.

Inside the main stone rampart, the people lived in circular stone-walled huts, of which several remnants survive. They now show up as circular depressions with a ring of stones sticking through the turf. The best have entrances and even a stone door post – see page 42.

Eighty years ago an excavation found evidence of fires, including charcoal pieces in the soil, but the best finds were pieces of iron slag that indicated a smelting furnace and the production of iron. The only other objects found were made of stone, including rubbing stones, part of a spindle whorl and large quantities of sling stones used to repel attackers.

The rubbing stones are river pebbles found in the huts and with one side flat and polished, so that they could be used for rubbing or grinding corn on saddle-shaped querns. The spindle whorl suggests that they were spinning flax grown in nearby marshy areas as well as wool. The site was disappointing because no pottery was found, and the dating of the settlement is still uncertain, although it was probably occupied in the first century AD.

Apart from the impressive stone wall and the entrance gate, the fields of pointed stones are its main feature. They are not found in any other hill-fort in north Wales, and are a remarkable feat of military engineering.

12. FIRES OF CELTIC RICHES
IRON AGE FIREDOG – CAPEL GARMON (GR 815550)

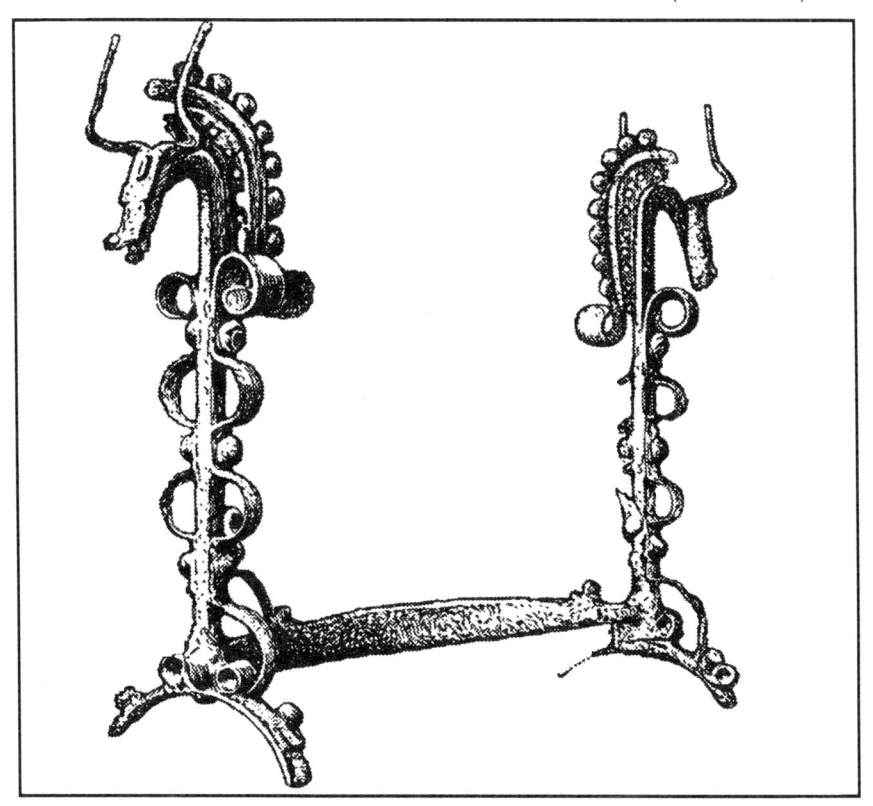

Late-Celtic Fire Dog found in a peat bog at Carreg Coediog, Capel Garmon.

Until the arrival of a comprehensive railway system to distribute coal, many farmers burnt peat that they cut during the summer months. In May 1852 a farmer near Capel Garmon was cutting a ditch when he found a wrought-iron firedog lying on its side, with a large stone placed at each end. The firedog rested on a clay floor and was hidden by a thick layer of peat, which had accumulated slowly in the bottom of a stagnant pool after the firedog had been placed there.

It was the custom in pre-Roman times to deposit objects in water as an offering or dedication as part of a water cult. Many objects have been found in mint condition in peat bogs, which suggest that they were placed there carefully and deliberately and sometimes over a period of two centuries. The most famous example in north Wales was the discovery of a vast collection of iron objects that included chains, swords and shields at Llyn Cerrig Bach in Ynys Môn.

In Capel Garmon the peat cover had excellently preserved the firedog and, although some corrosion is evident, it is the finest example in western Europe. Other examples have been found in eastern England (at Cambridge, Colchester and Welwyn for instance) and all are associated with other iron objects. These include cauldron rings and chains and suggest that the firedog was placed around a central hearth and used to hold cauldrons for cooking purposes.

The Capel Garmon firedog is 2 feet 10 inches (90cm) long and 2 feet (67cm) high and it consists of two vertical shafts and a connecting bar standing on semi-circular arched feet. The vertical shafts are bent over the top to form the horned head of an ox with a flowing mane resembling a helmet crest. The firedog was richly ornamented and shows that the aim of Celtic art was to beautify household and military equipment. It would have been at the centre of a hut occupied by a Celtic chief and was a symbol of wealth, style and prestige. In this fine example they made a stylistic representation of an animal so that the object appeared as fantasy rather than just a real object.

The Celtic smiths were famous throughout western Europe, in Germany, Switzerland and France, and used their skills to express their interest in magic and good luck. The smiths worked for an aristocratic patron and it is possible that the craft object would be made near the spot where it was found centuries later. By comparing it with the similar objects found in eastern England, it is possible to date the Capel Garmon firedog to the end of the Iron Age, and it was probably made locally about 50BC to 100AD. It is listed in the Catalogue of Iron Age Finds issued by the National Museum, Cardiff, where it is on display.

13. STONE SKELETONS OF THE HILLTOP HOMES
IRON AGE SETTLEMENT HUTS

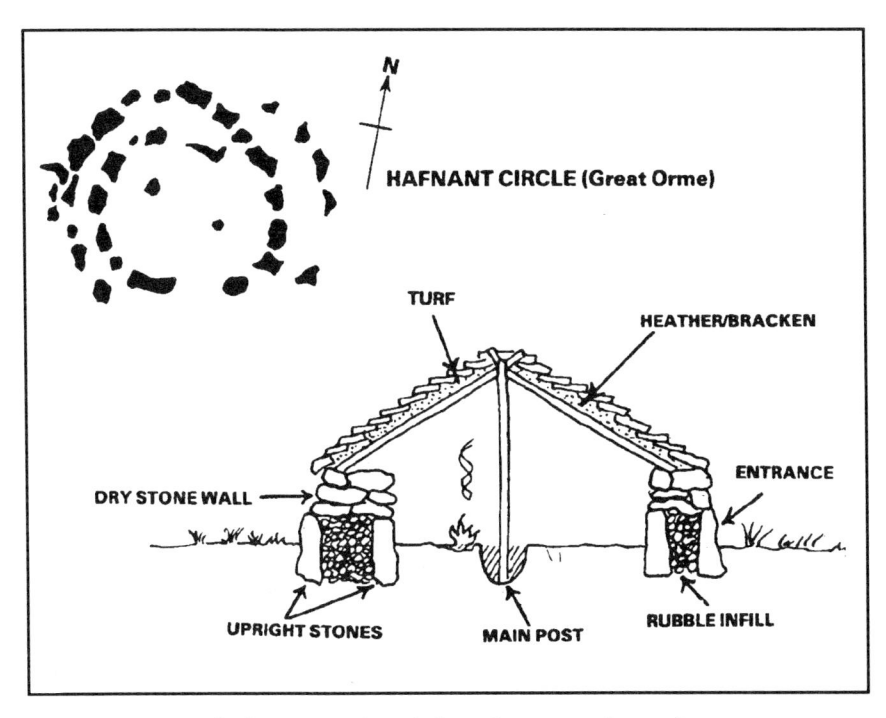

Jutting out of the moorland heather, circles of stones are a feature of Dyffryn Conwy's hill-tops. They are usually found in groups within an enclosing wall or bank, which would have given protection to the inhabitants and their domestic animals.

More than 300 of these circles are known in Gwynedd, but few have been excavated. The stones are the foundations of a wall 3-4 feet (90cm-1.2m) high, and this would have been the base of a timber and thatch 'wigwam' type structure large enough to house a family. Only the stones survive, but the plan and size show they were huts. The door, giving both ventilation and light, faced away from the prevailing westerly winds on the exposed hills. The two rows of stones was separated by an infill of rubble and earth.

Pen y Gaer - plan of circular hut

On the Y Gogarth *(the Great Orme)* are isolated examples of double walls of lime-stone sticking through the thin turf. One, at Hafnant to the south of Marine Drive, is 13 feet (4m) across with a double ring of limestone blocks a foot above the turf. The entrance, a yard (90cm) across, is on the sheltered south-east side and the views are spectacular.

The most striking huts, however, are from the hill forts such as Pen-y-gaer, Dinas and, further west, Tre'r Ceiri on Yr Eifl. Tre'r Ceiri has one hundred and fifty huts and finds include gold brooches, glass beads, bones, pottery and charcoal. Nothing earlier than AD130 was found, suggesting that Celtic/early Welsh people were in occupation during the Roman period.

The hut-circles generally have a much longer history, and were built by early farming people who lived in the hills centuries before the Romans. They grazed animals of the hills and used a simple wooden plough to grow wheat and oats in terraced fields. Traces of these terraced fields are to be found in the Cwm Tafalog above Ro-wen. As the plough was drawn along the slope, the soil moved to the downslope edge of the field, giving the appearance of a terrace.

These people used spindle whorls, suggesting wool and flax spinning, and querns and rubbing stones for grinding corn. The slopes were divided into small fields by stone walls that are now hardly visible. A few years ago a dig by the Archaeology Department of Clwyd County Council, at a site near Llyn Brenig in the Denbigh moors, exposed a thick layer of charcoal, thought to be the remains of domestic fires. Dating tests prove that the hut was lived in about 1000BC, the later part of the Bronze Age when the uplands of north Wales were warmer and drier.

Previously we had known about the Bronze Age from axes, swords, pottery and the burial mounds scattered over the hills. This identification of a farming community is an exceptionally valuable contribution to our knowledge of prehistoric times.

Tre Ceiri – hut

14. RIDDLE OF BOWL FROM THE GRAVE
(GR 948500)

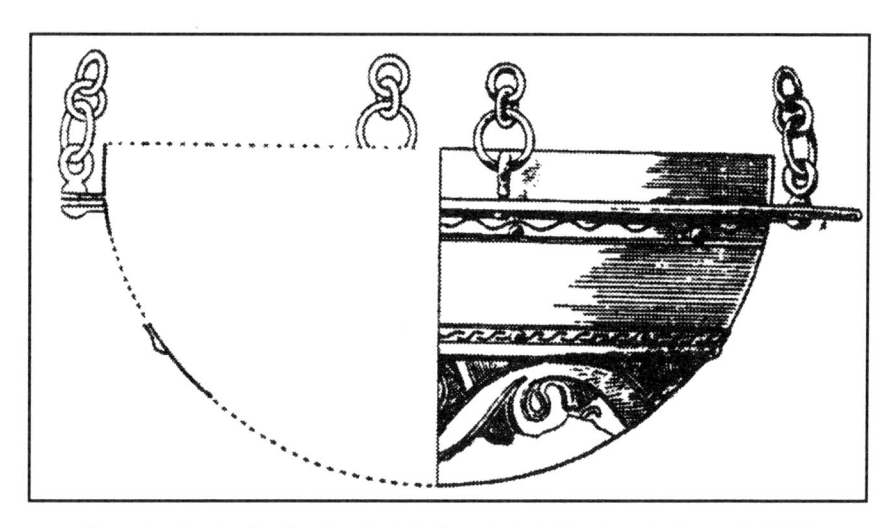

How the Cerrigydrudion bowl might have looked (Antiquaries Journal, 1926)

One of the strangest prehistoric finds in North Wales was a bronze object discovered in 1924 near Cerrigydrudion.

The farmer at Tŷ Tan-y-foel was digging for stone to repair a wall, and in the large field called Y Foel above a quarry he dislodged some slabs only a foot-and-a-half below the turf. The slabs and soil had collapsed into a grave or cist a long time before, and it's possible the grave had been robbed. In the soil he found curved pieces of a bronze dish or round-bottomed bowl. There were also four separate pieces of chain and a solid bronze ring. The longest chain was seven inches long and the bronze ring nearly one-and-a half inches in diameter. There were enough pieces to reconstruct the object which was catalogued as a "bronze hanging bowl" and sent to the National Museum at Cardiff.

Across the bowl there was a horizontal collar or flange to which the chains had originally been rivetted and then suspended from the solid bronze ring. In its day it would have been suspended from a roof beam and may have contained liquid as part of a ritual ceremony.

The most remarkable feature, found under the flange and on the base of the bow, was a well-preserved decoration engraved in the metal, or palm leaves of Celtic art and metalwork made before the Roman conquest of Britain. The Celts flourished in central Europe from Hungary to France and their greatest fame in this period (400-50BC) was their fine metalwork in iron, gold and bronze. Their cemeteries in Switzerland and Eastern France are rich in brooches, bracelets, neckrings and swords, which were buried with their leaders.

As they spread into North Wales, they brought their metal-working skills with them and many objects of iron work have been found. A shield found on Moel Hiraddug above Diserth has a strong Celtic design of scrolls and curves. They carried on their crafts of spinning, weaving iron working, pottery in their hill-top forts.

There have been finds of iron pellets, charcoal, crucibles, slag and iron ore deposits which point to a native smelting industry in this period known as the Iron Age. Although the find at Cerrigydrudion is random, there are six *cist* in the parish, and overlooking the village is the hill fort of Caer Caradog.

In 1980, the hanging bowl was sent from Cardiff on loan to the British Museum for an exhibition on the Gauls. The fragments were re-examined in the light of more recent knowledge and the idea that it was a hanging bowl has been challenged.

There were some differences in the designs shown on the bronze surfaces which suggested two separate vessels. Differences in the rivets were noticed and the wear on the rivets and rings was considerable, although the hanging bowl was a light-weight object. Even so, the bronze pieces were all cut from the same metal sheet and probably came from the same workshop.

The find may be the remains of two round lids finely decorated and fitting over the top of bronze vessels which have not survived, and which may have been removed from the cist by robbers at a later date. The lids would have fitted inside the rim of the missing vessels, and the decoration on the flange would have been on the upperside.

Some vessels in France have been found with lids attached by a chain, although the chains from Cerrigydrudion are exceptionally long. The exact purpose of the object found must remain a mystery, unless one with more pieces intact is found. Even so, the Cerrigydrudion bowl is one of the finest and most important pieces of Celtic art and metalwork found in Britain.

15. COIN TRAIL LEFT CLUES TO INVADER
ROMAN COINS (GR 815820)

Roman coins have been found in great numbers in north Wales, and those in mint or fine condition are of first-rate importance to the historian. Each Roman mint had its own distinctive stamp, so apart from the dates and their dedication to ruling emperors, it's also possible to identify the mint in Italy, France or Britain where the coins were struck.

The faces of a Constantine coin found on the Orme.

Apart from Canovium (Caerhun), the most concentrated area for finds was along the coastal strip between Colwyn Bay and Abergele. Another was across the narrow pass over the western slope of the *Little Orme*, now followed by the main road to Llandudno.

Consignments of coins were sent from Chester in boxes or jars, but some did not reach their destination being sometimes lost, stolen or hidden in secret places along this route. This accounts for the number of hoards that have been found, including one of five thousand coins discovered in Penrhyn Bay in 1873 although the container, an earthenware jar, was not opened until 1903. The brass coins were mainly minted in London with the stamp PLON or PLN clearly visible on most of them. They were struck in the reign of Constantine the Great about AD310. It is significant that they were found on the prehistoric route from Dinas hill-fort on the Great Orme to the hill-fort at Bryn Euryn (Colwyn Bay). Some of the coins were in uncirculated condition of the highest design and workmanship, and were probably on their way from Chester when the consignment was intercepted and hidden. In his pre-Christian days, Constantine favoured the cult of Sol (the Sun), which appears on the reverse side of the coins.

Half-a-mile (800m) up the road, near the head of the pass over the Little Orme, another hoard was found at the foot of the crags in the winter of 1907. This hoard contained five hundred and fifty coins and an associated bronze plate suggested that they were held in a box or a leather bag. These were also brass coins issued by the London mint a few years earlier than the larger hoard, in AD289 to AD293, during the rule of the Separatist Emperor Carausius.

Smaller hoards of coins of this period, also dedicated to Constantine, were found in an urn at Llys Euryn and another at Rhos Fynach where six coins were wrapped in a sheet of lead and buried in the abbey garden. Isolated finds include one coin at Nant Sember, one south of Gogarth Hall, one at Graig Lwyd quarry, Penmaenmawr; and another at Aber, where a coin of Constantine was found. Further evidence was a hoard of seventeen coins found at Kendrick's Cave just below Dinas hill-fort near Llandudno

Apart from the coastal routeway, the main finds of Roman coins were made at Canovium where a fort existed from AD70 to AD410. Hundreds of coins have been unearthed over the past three hundred years, most of them being isolated finds belonging to the former inhabitants.

These finds were particularly valuable between 1926 and 1932 when the fort was excavated because they were used to date buildings and roads inside the fort. They include early coins brought over from Italy, some as early as 38BC, and they range to coins from as late as AD410, when the Roman garrison withdrew.

The chance discovery of a hoard of coins is interesting but not as useful as the isolated finds found during the process of excavation, which can be used in interpreting the full history of the site. When Sir Mortimer Wheeler found a mint coin in the mortar of a wall at Caernarfon, he said: 'Its evidence is at once certain and precise; the building was erected within a few years of AD350.'

16. MILESTONE LEGACY OF THE ROMANS
ROMAN MILESTONES (GR 718716/677730)

When going on a journey today, we can phone the RAC or AA to get information about the most suitable route, about interesting towns en route, about distances from place to place, about any tolls we are likely to have to pay and also, unfortunately, about possible bottlenecks or diversions.

In Roman times, around AD200, they consulted the Antonine Itinerary, which was a road book giving all the main towns, forts, roads and distances in Roman miles. From the legionary base at Chester (Deva) they would have used Route Eleven, called Iter XI, to Caernarfon (Segontium) which was the most distant fort in north Wales lying seventy-three Roman miles from Chester. An important stop on the way was the fort at Caerhun (Canovium) in Dyffryn Conwy.

Replica of a Roman milestone found above Rhiwiau Uchaf

The fort can be seen in aerial photographs as a perfect square-shaped outline, with the 13th century church of Caerhun tucked away in the north-west corner of the fort. The fort is now largely hidden under the grass and tree-covered parkland, the church itself and the graveyard, but there are still clearly visible remains of the outer bank and the gates. Also, just outside the fort towards Afon Conwy, there are remains of the Roman stone-built jetty and a large bath-house. The Romans often used the old Celtic names and in this case Canovium derived from the Celtic/old Welsh name 'Conwy'.

From Canovium the Roman road ran west to the high pass of Bwlch y Ddeufaen separating the mountain ridges of Drum and

Tal-y-fan. If you mention the Roman road at the picturesque village of Ro-wen at the foot of the pass, villagers will point out traces of it as a sunken depression, a terrace cut in the hillside or a patch of rough paving.

This section through Bwlch y Ddeufaen has been accepted as the finest example of a Roman road in Gwynedd since the 1840's, but the first positive proof came during the winter of 1883.

In February 1883 farmworkers draining a marshy field on the slope above Rhiwiau Uchaf, south of Llanfairfechan, were astonished to find a huge cylindrical stone that had fallen into the marsh. Removing the stone, which stood at nearly 7 feet (2.1m) tall, they found that a clear Latin inscription had survived on the upper face of the stone.

Today, just above the derelict farmhouse, a gate in the wall leads to a modern concrete replica of the stone that had replaced the original, which now stands in the British Museum. The translated inscription reads:

EMPEROR CAESAR TRAJAN HADRIAN AUGUSTUS, PONTIFEX MAXIMUS, IN HIS FIFTH YEAR OF TRIBUNICAL POWER, FATHER OF HIS COUNTRY, THRICE CONSUL: FROM KANOVIUM 8 MILES.

It is a self-proclaimed Roman milestone dedicated to Emperor Hadrian and one of the finest ever found in Britian. The fifth year of Hadrian's tribunical power was AD 120-121 so that the exact date of the setting up of the stone is known as well as the exact distance – eight miles – from the fort at Canovium.

This imposing column was made of the finest quality stone – a hard sandstone with small quartz pebbles that may have come from Minera near Wrexham. It would have been brought to the legionary base at Chester and then dressed and professionally inscribed at the legionary workshops before being shipped direct to Canovium. It was then carried over Bwlch y Ddeufaen to be set up at eight Roman miles from Canovium, and was probably one of a series.

This spectacular archaeological find was followed by the

amazing discovery of another milestone only five months later in the same field. This one was dedicated to Emperor Septimius Severus (AD198-209) and set up near Hadrian's stone about eighty years later. A slate tablet records that an aqueduct supplying water to Segontium was rebuilt by Severus thus indicating that the fort there was refurbished in the reign of Septimius Severus;. It is therefore possible that the road over Bwlch y Ddeufaen was also repaired at this time and a new milestone dedicated to Severus was set up to replace the eighty year old Hadrianic stone which was unceremoniously pushed into the marsh. The Severus stone is also a quartz-pebble sandstone, cylindrical in form, but remains only as a fragment. The evidence of increased activity at Segontium, and perhaps an increase in the garrison may have led to the resurfacing of this vital supply road from Canovium to Segontium.

Roman Milestone (Hadrian) above Llanfairfechan

No further discoveries were made until May 1954 when a Roman milestone was found almost completely embedded in peat on Bwlch y Ddeufaen. The find was made on Wednesday, May 19, 1954 by three members of

Roman Milestone (Constantine) in Bwlch y Ddeufaen Pass

51

Roman Road in Bwlch y Ddeufaen

the local history society. They noticed a fragment of dressed stone protruding through the turf and, when they lifted it out, Frank Jowett noticed a clearly legible inscription on the protected underside of the slab. The stone was about 2 feet (60cm) high with $2^1/_2$ inch (6.5cm) letters. It was of a local volcanic rock.

The stone eventually reached Dr Nash Williams of the National Museum of Wales, an expert on inscribed stones, who translated the stone as 'Son Of The Divine Constantinus, Pius Augustus' and then identified it as a Roman milestone set up by Emperor Constantine (AD 306-337) the son of Constantinius. It was therefore much later than the stones found at Rhiwiau and proved that the Romans were still using the road over Bwlch y Ddeufaen in the 4th century.

This milestone was exactly five miles from Canovium and again probably in its original position, though it remained undiscovered until 1954 because its inscribed side had fallen face down into the peat. There are many stones scattered over the slopes and only chance and sharp observation would have detected this one. An unusual insect sunning itself on the slab was first noticed and then as they inspected it, one of the party realised that the stone was dressed. They managed to make a bag for the stone using strong twine left behind by a farmer and transported it in turns to the bus stop at Ro-wen. They managed to persuade the bus driver to allow them to take it on board, and it was then taken to Cardiff, where it remains on display in the National Museum. A grid reference to its location was recorded in the official papers but, unlike the Hadrianic stone at Rhiwiau, no replica stone was ever placed at the exact find-spot on this bleak pass.

Apart from being of interest in themselves as historical relics, milestones always add further clues to the exact course of the roads which the Romans built to link their forts. The latest find in Gwynedd was made in 1959, when another milestone was found in its original position near Madryn Farm, west of Llanfairfechan. It is made of igneous rock, probably from the nearby Tal-y-fan ridge, and was found by the farmer ploughing a field to the east of the farm. His plough turned up a large stone, all of 5 feet 10 inches (1.7m) high, and he fortunately noticed that it had an inscription on the flat side of the stone.

After cleaning, carelessly-cut capital letters could be read and it was identified as being dedicated to Emperor Postumus in the fourth year of his tribunician power. This dates the stone exactly to the year AD262. It must have stood on the side of the road from Canovium to Segontium, and is spaced one Roman mile from the Hadrianic stone at Rhiwiau. Altogether over the years, six milestones have been found in Gwynedd, all on or near to this road. This makes Gwynedd one of the most fruitful areas in Britain for such finds, and suggests it could yield yet more reminders of Roman involvement in the region.

17. SECRETS OF THE BATHS UNEARTHED IN SEARCH FOR THE EMPIRE'S BURIED TREASURE
ROMAN BATHS (CAERHUN) (GR 776705)

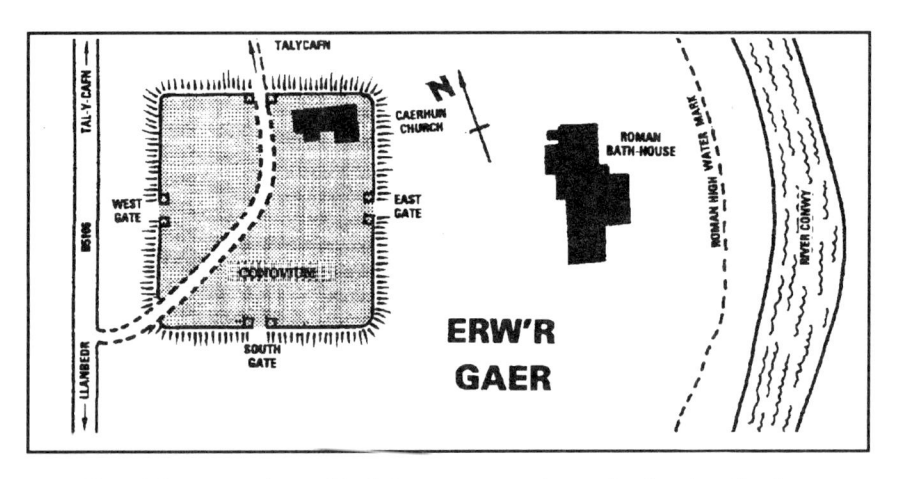

Plan of the Roman fort and bath-houses excavated near the church at Caerhun.

The Romans had a small but imposing fort at Caerhun that they called Canovium. It stood on a high bank overlooking Afon Conwy so that it could control the river crossing as well as the road over Bwlch y Ddeufaen, the pass between Tal-y-fan and Drum to Segontium (the modern Caernarfon).

The best view is from the opposite bank of the Conwy on the layby below the wooded slopes of Tan'rallt, 1 mile (1.6km) south of Tal-y-cafn. The A470 has been straightened in this section and the fragment of the old road that was left makes a perfect viewing point for the Roman fort. On a Sunday morning the church bells peal across the salt marsh from the 13th century church of Caerhun, neatly sited in the corner of the Roman Fort.

From Tan'rallt the Roman wall is a clearly visible rampart of earth, with a stone facing and a rubble core, which has survived intact for nearly two thousand years. Below the wall there is a steep slope towards the river with a small hillock and adjoining

Hypocaust system

bank, which was the scene of lively and enthusiastic excavation in July 1801. This is the site of a Roman bath-house that consisted of a group of inter-connected rooms, passages and steps. The baths were a short walk towards the river from the fort. Such bath-houses were often situated just outside the walls of a Roman fort with a source of water above and a slope below to carry the drainage to the river meadows.

Today the site is a grass-covered mound running in a line along the slope and marked by the stumps of trees. In Bezant Lowe's Heart of North Wales, a 1913 photograph shows a clearly-defined wall being penetrated by tree roots. These trees survived as late as 1940, and there were reports of pottery and bricks being dislodged by roots. The trees were felled and the site grassed over; therefore some imagination is now needed! Below this mound the slope falls to the flood plain and tidal marsh bordering Afon Conwy. It is difficult today to recognise this mid-slope bank as a place at which Roman soldiers and their families would have enjoyed a leisurely bath.

The bath-house would have had a cold room, a warm room, a hot room and a cold plunge-pool. The hollow space under the floor of the hot and warm rooms would have been supported by 2 foot (60cm) square tiles piled one upon another to form pillars and, at the corners, brick pillars. Into this space under the floor the hot air was funnelled in from an outside furnace and temperatures raised to an even 22°C. The furnace would be stoked with brushwood and charcoal. Hollow tiles in the walls and vents would allow the air to circulate. The pillars and bricks, some of which were hollow, have been known to be at Caerhun since 1580.

In 1807 Samuel Lysons, who was a noted archaeologist of his era, drew a plan of the fort. The bath-house was in the field below, known as Erw'r Gaer (Fort Acre). He had dug the site in 1801 and had no difficulty persuading the labourers, many of whom were spared from hay-making and were well acquainted with the tradition that the adjoining wooded plot was the site of treasure. Lysons drew a plan and described the excavation of twelve rooms some of which had plaster walls. He noted that bricks and tiles were found everywhere. He was very impressed by the square-tiled hypocaust system, similar as the one found in Bridge Street, Chester. The floors were paved with slate and in places steps badly worn by use led from one room to the next. Drains were found under the floors and all the excavated evidence indicated a complex of rooms forming a bath-house.

Nearly 2000 years is a long time for a modest building like this to survive; but the site can still be clearly seen from this special roadside viewpoint at Tan'rallt.

18. SHEEP REPLACE SOLDIERS IN THE FORT WITH NO NAME
ROMAN FORT – BRYN GEFEILIAU (GR 745573)

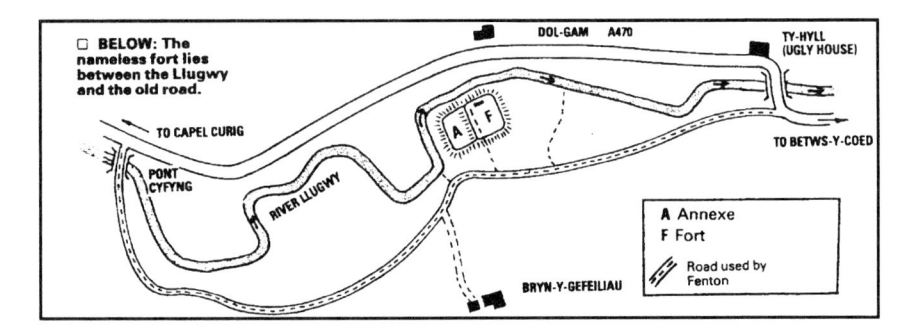

```
☐ BELOW: The
  nameless fort lies
  between the Llugwy
  and the old road.
```

Map labels: DOL-GAM A470, TY-HYLL (UGLY HOUSE), TO CAPEL CURIG, TO BETWS-Y-COED, PONT CYFYNG, RIVER LLUGWY, BRYN-Y-GEFEILIAU

Legend:
A Annexe
F Fort
Road used by Fenton

Two flat fields that lie within a broad loop of Afon Llugwy at the foot of Moel Siabod do not, at first sight, suggest a Roman fort. The fields belong to the hillside farm of Bryn Gefeiliau and are grazed by sheep, but there are records of hay-making on these wet meadows, and even of grain harvesting.

The fort was established about AD80 but, unlike the larger neighbour of Canovium (Caerhun), its official name is not known. Its existence, however, was known to Edward Lhuyd, who mentioned it in his Parochialia at the end of the 17th century. In 1807 Samuel Lysons referred to:
'considerable remains of a Roman building at Bryn Gefeiliau, walls and several short pillars of stone like those of the hypocaust under the Feathers Inn, Chester'.

This positive statement attracted the travel writer Richard Fenton to visit the site and his diary gives a vivid account of the evidence as it stood in the summer of 1810. In Fenton's day the road from Betws-y-coed went past the Rhaeadr Ewynnol (now erroneously known as the Swallow Falls) and along the southern side of Afon Llugwy to Pont Gyfyng, and then on to Capel Curig. This road is now a narrow lane, deserted by the modern traffic that passes over Pont Tŷ Hyll and past the front of the eponymous well-known house.

Bryn y Gefeiliau Roman Fort near Capel Curig

The old road runs past the remains of the Roman fort which, despite centuries of ploughing, survives with sections of its clay ramparts, built over a core of rubble, still visible. The rampart of the fort is the typical 'playing card' shape with three gates and a ditch separating it from another square enclosure called the 'annexe'. The fort and annexe are now only just above high flood levels.

A large mound of stones in the annexe was excavated in 1920-22, revealing a large building with walls standing to 4 feet (1.2m) above floor levels. In places, five courses of masonry were exposed. The floor itself was made of irregular slabs of dressed slate that had been squared by being sawn and then broken. A drain was found 18 inches (45cm) below the floor.

Another wing was found, this one with three rooms, as was much pottery including a shattered 30 inch (80cm) high amphora that was later successfully restored. Only one coin was found, of Emperor Domitian who ruled from AD80 to AD90, and this was a useful clue to the date of the building of this small fort in Eryri.

Since 1922 no further archaeological evidence has come to light but there is plenty of un-excavated land that might eventually, perhaps by ploughing or through a natural disturbance such as a flood, yield further Roman artefacts. With careful observation many pieces of coarse pottery, bricks and tiles can be seen on the surface of the meadow. A mole, in the process of building a molehill, recently caused a 'small find' in the form of a blue-glass melon bead that came to light in the north-west corner of the fort. Such blue-glass beads are common on Roman military sites and many were found in the larger fort of Canovium (Caerhun). This was also the fort through which supplies to Bryn Gefeiliau were brought by road. However the glass bead did not match any of those found in Canovium, but an exact match was found at the small fort at Penyllystyn, on the western edge of Eryri and at the limit of Roman occupation in north Wales. These two matching beads are royal blue in colour, hand-made with fourteen ribs or crimps. The diameter is 22mm and, although slightly worn, the fire-polish is still visible. Both were probably made at the same time in northern Italy in the latter half of the first century AD and exported to all parts of the Roman Empire, from Egypt to Scotland. It is not uncommon to find a few displayed in museums and it is thought that the vivid blue colour was considered a protection against evil. A detailed excavation at Penyllystyn, that was made before the whole site of the fort was removed for gravel extraction, concluded that the fort there may only have lasted from AD80 to AD90, so that the blue bead at Bryn Gefeiliau may also belong to that date. Even as small a find as a bead, although not as valuable as a coin, can add to the history of a site.

Today the excavated area is a mound of loose rocks, trees and bushes, but Fenton and other eye-witnesses were convinced that an elaborate bath-house with a hypocaust heating system had once existed here. Richard Fenton stayed in Capel Curig in July 1810, and came almost daily to visit the fort in the hope of finding Roman evidence. Fenton's friend, the artist Richard Colt-Hoare, accompanied him on these visits and sketched the buildings in the annexe. Many of his sketches of famous views, such as Snowdon from Capel Curig, have been published in book form or are kept in the National Library of Wales in Aberystwyth and others in Cardiff Library. His less well-known sketches of Wales may be found in a collection at the family home at Stourhead in Wiltshire. It is therefore possible that a sketch made at Bryn Gefeiliau on July 14, 1810 may still exist. An entry in Colt-Hoare's diary for that day states: 'sketched the wall of the little enclosure with six or seven rude stone pillars that divided the upper and lower storeys of the hypocaust of a building which was a luxury attached to every villa of the Romans'. This was the same building that was identified three years earlier by Samuel Lysons, and compared by him to the famous hypocaust at the Feathers Inn in Chester, part of which is now under that well known purveyor of potatoes, Spud-u-like! The rest of the Feathers Inn was demolished in 1863. The building at Bryn Gefeiliau was probably the fort's bath-house or part of the heated 'villa' of the commandant.

Roman beads found at Bryn y Gefeiliau

In his diary, Fenton claims that the fort had been a centre for smelting iron and for forging tools and implements. 'There are plenty of fragments of iron slag to be found all over the hills around Bryn Gefeiliau.' It is possible that the fort and its annexe made use of the local iron and lead deposits. With careful field observation, it is still possible to find fragments of iron slag on the hills, as in Fenton's day.

19. STONY SECRETS OF DARK AGES
EARLY CHRISTIAN STONES – PENMACHNO (GR 790506)

Little is known about the Dark Ages in Dyffryn Conwy (400-800 AD) after the withdrawal of the Romans, apart from the missionary activity of the Celtic saints. These saints preached the Christian message and set up wooden cells, with an enclosing wall called a 'llan'. Many towns and villages can therefore trace their origins to this period and are named after travelling saints such as Tudno, Crwst, Celynin and others.

Early Christian Stone at Penmachno

Our main sources of information to this period are the engraved tombstones, of which thirty have been found in north Wales. They are slabs of stone in their natural, undressed state, 2 to 5 feet (60cm to 1.9m) long, which are notable because they bear an inscription. This often records the name of the deceased person and other information that can be used to fix a date.

The finest collection of these stones was found in Penmachno and now lie in a splendid niche in St Tudclud's parish church.

The best-known stone is the Carausius Stone. The stone is dedicated to Carausius, who 'lies under these stones' and has a Christian monogram (the Greek letters XP) representing the first two letters of 'Christ'.

This stone is likely to have been set up in the late 5th or early 6th century at a time when Christianity was first beginning in this corner of the country. It is the earliest archaeological evidence of Christianity in north Wales, and obviously commemorates a person of some importance.

All the stones are written in Latin and the words suggest contacts between the early Welsh church and the Christians of Southern Gaul, in what was probably the area now known as the Rhone Valley.

Another stone of the same age refers to Cantorius who was a citizen of Venedos, which was the Latin name for Gwynedd. Another stone records the name of the son of Avitorius, which was set up in the time of Justinus the Consul. This stone clearly shows the link between the churches of Wales and Gaul because inscribed stones found in the area around the city of Lyons also refer to the consuls reigning at the time the tombstones were set up. Historical evidence shows that Justinus held the consulship in 540 AD, so that gives a positive date to the Avitorius stone in Penmachno church.

These valuable stones, originally found in and around Penmachno, are a worthy record of our history. Fortunately they have remained in the area where they originally stood and they now add an extra reward to visiting the splendid church at Penmachno.

20. RINGING LEGACY FROM A VALLEY'S INVADING SAINT
'CELTIC BELL' – DOLWYDDELAN (GR 736522)

A Celtic bell from around the seventh century hangs from the nave roof at the church of St Gwyddel in Dolwyddelan. A portable bell, it is one of only six in Wales, and was found in 1850 on the site of a nearby stone church at Bryn-y-Bedd.

Christianity was slowly introduced to Wales following the withdrawal of the Romans by what are popularly known today as 'Celtic saints'. Many settled along Cardigan Bay before pushing inland to set up their missionary 'colonies'. St Gwyddel is said to have arrived at Dolwyddelan in about AD600, and set up his preaching cross – the first sign of his missionary purpose – on the hill called Bryn-y-Bedd, 300 yards (270m) west of the present church. Soon afterwards a wooden church was built on this 'hill of graves', but all that has survived from this period is the old Saints' Celtic bell.

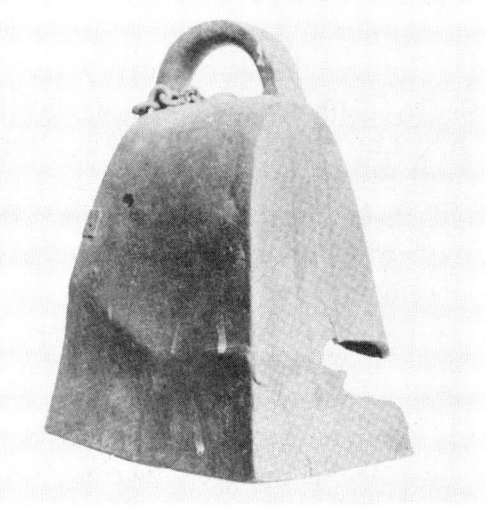

Celtic Bell in Dolwyddelan Church

The small wooden church remained the centre of religious activity in Dyffryn Lledr (valley) until the 12th century, when a stone church was built on the original foundation. This survived until 1500 when Maredudd ap Ieuan, who lived in Castell Dolwyddelan, built a new church in a more open position. It was considered to be better placed to reduce the risk of attack from bandits who had made their stronghold in the hospice at nearby Ysbyty Ifan. It is recorded that when Maredudd went to church he was accompanied by a bodyguard of twenty, and that he posted a lookout on the top of a neighbouring hill, Carreg Alltrem, to warn him of any impending ambush.

Brasses in the church commemorate Maredudd, who was also the founder of the Wynne 'dynasty' at Gwydir. To build the new church he used some of the stone materials and fittings from the old church, and fragments of old glass in the east window of St Gwyddel's Church date from 1512.

There is no record of the old Celtic bell until 1850, when it was found on the site of the old church at Bryn-y-Bedd. It is made of iron/sheet, and the original handle for swinging the bell is intact, despite damage to other parts. The plate has been hammered into shape, rivetted down the side and dipped into bronze to prevent corrosion. It has four flat sides, like all Celtic bells, and is 8 inches (20.3cm) high. It would have been used by Gwyddel and his followers as a portable bell, for fixed bells were not a feature of the early Celtic church in Wales.

The portable bells were brought to Wales by the Celtic saints from Ireland, where sixty still exist. They include St Patrick's own bell (although he went to Ireland from Wales), which is referred to in literature and is now, nearly a millennium and a half later, on display at the National Museum in Dublin.

In the Celtic world, these bells were highly esteemed, and not just to summon the scattered population of the valleys and hills to pray. They were regarded with veneration and awe; they were thought to possess magic powers, and were even used to cure illnesses. The Celtic bells continued in use down to the 12th century, when stone churches with external bell-cotes in the Norman/Roman tradition replaced them.

21. CONQUERORS' FIRST FOOTHOLD
MOTTE AND BAILEY CASTLE (ABER) (GR 796566)

Hill of Mud: the name hardly entices the visitor, and the mound is now partly hidden by the houses of Aber village. But in its day the Norman building on the 100-foot (30.5m) contour would have had commanding views across Traeth Lafan to Ynys Môn.

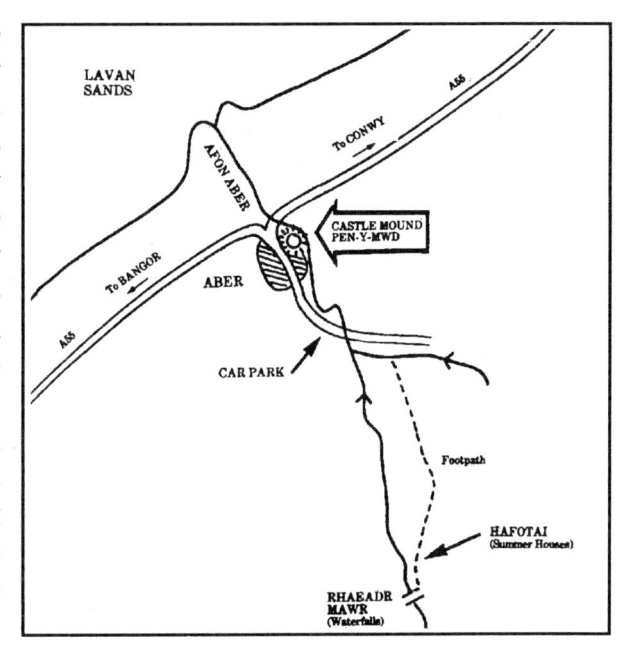

A flat-topped motte, or circular mound, rises abruptly 22 feet (6.8m) from the meadow of Afon Aber. Leland, writing in the 16th century, said that parts of a building still stood, and Pennant claimed in 1790 that some foundations could still be seen. But today, the only evidence of a building on the flat-topped surface is one flat slab sticking through the turf.

The sides of the motte are steep, and on the southern side is a ditch that provided building material for the mound. The bulk of the motte consists of large river-worn boulders collected from the nearby Afon Aber, and these are embedded in layers of gravel, clay and sand.

The builders used the new method of building a motte shown in the Bayeux Tapestry. It shows workmen using shovels and picks digging out a ditch; the slopes of the motte were

The mound's top is still perfectly flat

steeply graded and the summit levelled so accurately that even today it is as flat as a billiard table. It would have been surrounded by a timber stockade. The motte at Aber is similar to other early Norman mounds.

The Normans gained a foothold along the north Wales coast soon after 1066 and the Earls of Chester went on to set up motte and bailey castles at Caernarfon, Bangor and Aberlleiniog. However, they abandoned Gwynedd in 1098 when Gruffydd ap Cynan returned as its prince; and the Normans did not return as settlers for the next two hundred years. It is possible that Hugh d'Avranches, Earl of Chester, built the motte at Aber during this brief period of Norman advance, although there is no documentary evidence for its date.

By 1100, the Welsh princes had taken over the site and it became a llys, royal hall called Tŷ Hir or Long House. Aber became the centre of the commote of Arllechwedd Uchaf and the seat of the Prince of Gwynedd. It was a favoured residence of Llywelyn Fawr (the Great). His wife, Siwan/Joan, died here in 1237 and was buried at the Franciscan convent at Llanfaes, a little to the east of where Edward 1 was to build his castle and English town at Beaumaris. The carved stone lid of her coffin is now in the porch of Beaumaris church.

Llywelyn's palace has disappeared but the motte has survived. The only damage to it has been from tree roots, which have exposed a few valuable sections into its boulder and earth structure.

22. HOLY MEN USED TO HARD WORK
ABERCONWY ABBEY (CONWY) (GR 782776)

In summer, Conwy is crowded with people, yet 800 years ago it was 'far from the haunts of men'. It was hemmed in by Conwy mountain, by Afon Gyffin, and by the tidal estuary and the sand dunes along the coast. This splendid isolation was the reason that, in 1188, the Cistercian monks chose it for their new abbey at Aberconwy.

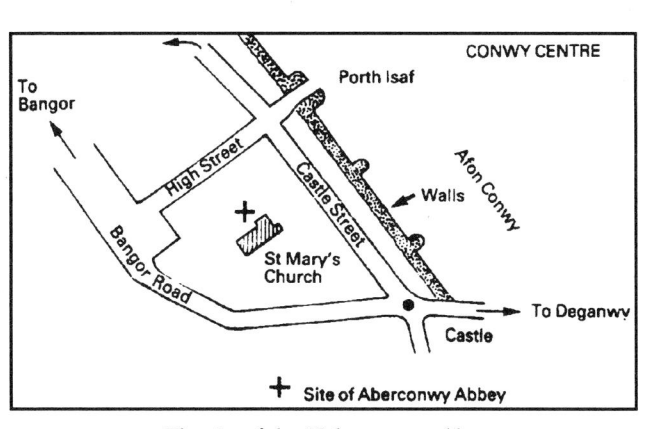

The site of the 12th-century abbey

The famous traveller, Geraldus Cambrensis, on his way from Bangor in 1188 waited for low tide to get round Penmaen Bach, passed the abbey 'on my right side' and crossed Afon Conwy by ferry. He was travelling with Archbishop Baldwin, and they were on a recruiting drive for the Crusade.

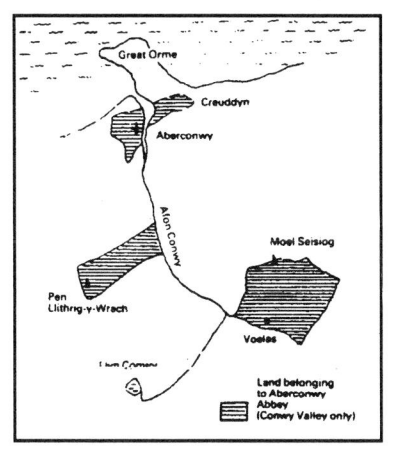

The abbey's lands in the Conwy Valley

The rocky outcrop was granted to the monks by Gruffudd ap Cynan, King of Gwynedd, and he was buried in a monk's cowl in the abbey. Llywelyn Fawr granted the monks extensive lands and further privileges in 1198. The charter was written in Latin, but Welsh place-names were also recorded. Across Afon Conwy they were given land in Creuddyn, where wheat was grown between Deganwy and Bodysgallen and meadows provided hay. On the hills above Dolgarrog and Pentrefoelas they could graze sheep in the summer. These lands were all within a day's journey of the abbey, but were worked by lay brothers who lived on the granges and had their own chapel. They also wore black cloaks so as to distinguish them from the white-robed monks.

The Cistercians were working monks, who believed in making their monasteries self-sufficient. Sheep and cattle provided material for shoes, tunics and cowls. They didn't eat flesh-meat, and depended on catching fish from Afon Conwy and Afon Gyffin, and may have used a fish weir at Llandrillo-yn-Rhos (Rhos-on-Sea). There are records of a monk praying daily for the success of the fishery in a stone cell near a spring or well at Rhos, and there are records of the abbot buying fishing nets at Chester in 1258.

They were given the right to recover cargoes wrecked off their shoreline; and these in themselves supplied them with wine, honey and sometimes gold and silver. The monastery was also a small factory with fulling mills to produce wool, looms for weaving cloth, a well, a fish-pond and a bake-house. Corn was ground there for bread, flax was made into linen for altar cloths, and hay was stored for the winter months.

They were exempt from tolls and taxes and had their own system of law. The abbot had to go to the Cistercian 'headquarters' at Citeaux in eastern France once a year for the Chapter of the Order. The Cistercians were popular in Wales because of their attachment to manual work; and they were strongly identified with the poor.

When Edward I conquered Wales, he did not want an abbey near his castle, and within the walls of his new town, at Conwy. He had it moved in 1282 upstream to Maenan, but granted all the lands and privileges previously given in the 1198 Charter. Little remains of the original abbey of Aberconwy except for parts of the fabric of St Mary's church, built in the grounds of the old abbey.

23. A STONE KNIGHT STAYS ON GUARD AFTER 600 YEARS
EFFIGY – BETWS-Y-COED (GR 596 566)

In an arch in St Michael's church on the river bank at Betws-y-coed is a stone effigy of a medieval knight in full military uniform. Similar figures can be found in other churches in Eryri. In St Cadfan's Church at Tywyn, Meirionnydd, for instance, is an effigy of Gruffudd ap Adda of Dolgoch who died in 1331.

The effigy at Betws-y-coed is in fine condition, and may have lain undisturbed for 600 years. The Latin inscription says it is the effigy of Gruffudd ap Dafydd Goch. His grandfather was Dafydd, natural brother of Llywelyn ap Gruffudd, the last Prince of Wales. It is mentioned that Gruffudd lived in the isolated house of Fedw Deg, which still stands in the hills above Penmachno. He was foreman of the jury in 1352 at Trefriw, where he owned land, and he also had arable land near Penmachno.

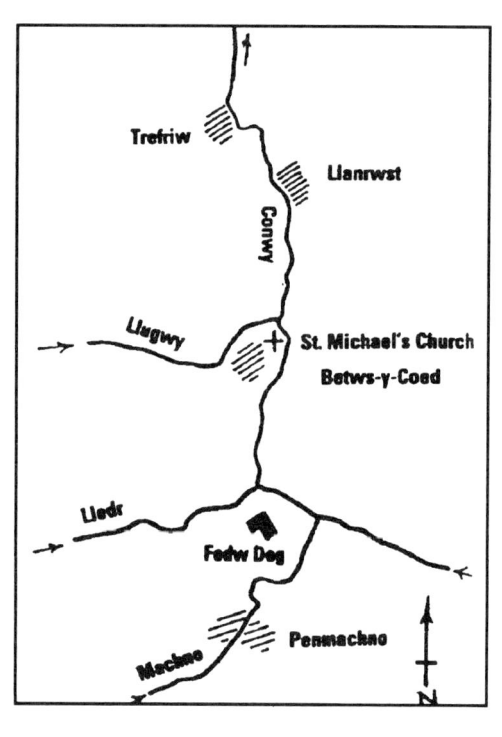

The effigy is carved in fine quality limestone, probably by the renowned Welsh sculptors of north Flintshire. They provided the freestone carvings and sculptures for the many churches and abbeys that were built at this time. Nothing is known about the transport of such large blocks, but they were probably brought

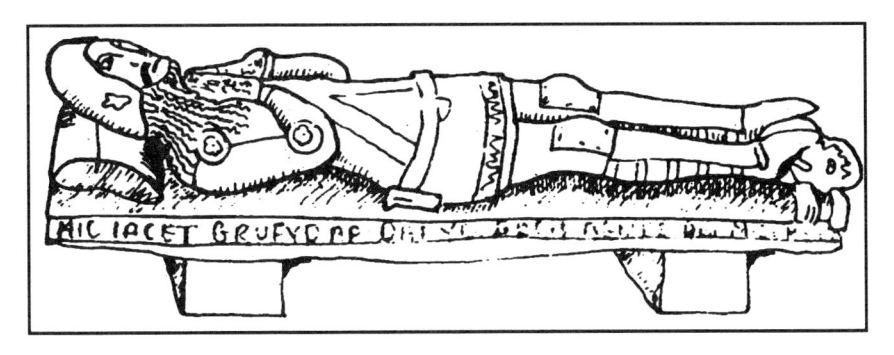

The massive stone figure of Gruffudd ap Dafydd Goch at St Michael's Church

by raft up Afon Conwy to the church at the river's edge.

The effigy of Gruffudd in the chancel wall is of a knight in the full armour of the late 14th century because chain mail gave way to plate armour about 1350-1385. It is similar to that worn by the Black Prince on his effigy in Canterbury Cathedral, and is very similar to the effigy at Llanuwchllyn Church, near Bala, which has the date 1395 inscribed on it. The knight at Betws-y-coed is 6'8" (2m) long, lying flat on a slab of limestone with its head enclosed by a conical helmet. Neck and shoulders are protected by rings of chain mail; the hands are in plated gauntlets and the body under a coat of plate. On top of this is a sleeveless 'pullover' of thin material. A belt, with a coat of arms made up of a chevron and two oak leaves, holds a sword, and a dagger for a final thrust. The carver would have used the latest armour and added some individual features such as a moustache and beard.

The effigy was probably carved between 1380 and 1385, near the end of the golden age of carving in North Wales. Gruffudd was one of the knights who fought under the Black Prince in the French wars under Edward III. He returned afterwards to the family house at Fedw Deg, which still stands six hundred years later on the ridge above the Lledr Valley. It was in a partly-ruined condition when it was leased to the Forestry Commission but, together with the effigy at St Michael's, it provides an interesting glimpse of medieval times.

24. VANISHING CASTLE BUILT FROM DUNES
MEDIEVAL CASTLE – CWM PRYSOR (GR 758369)

A view of what remains of Castell Prysor from the A4212

My first reaction when I saw the castle was one of disbelief. I had come through Ysbyty Ifan, over Y Migneint to Cwm Prysor. As the road drops steeply from the Migneint, the open moors are replaced by neat, walled fields. The map showed a castle a few yards from the A4212. Castell Prysor was a conical hill rising above Afon Prysor, and, from the road, seemed to have a thick cover of loose rock.

It was hard to believe that this was a castle. The stream and fence prevented direct access from the road, so I took the farm road and met the farmer who owned the castle. He stated that it was 'just a ruin, a pile of stones, although it is a scheduled monument and I have to avoid damaging its structure'. He generously invited me to look around, but warned that the stonework was loose and overgrown by small trees and bushes.

My main purpose was to see if any layers of masonry and even mortar had survived the centuries. The conical mound is a motte built on a natural outcrop of rock then raised and strengthened by layers of stone. There is plenty of slate and volcanic rock on the nearby hills, but any sand and lime for mortar would have been brought in from the dunes and beach near Harlech.

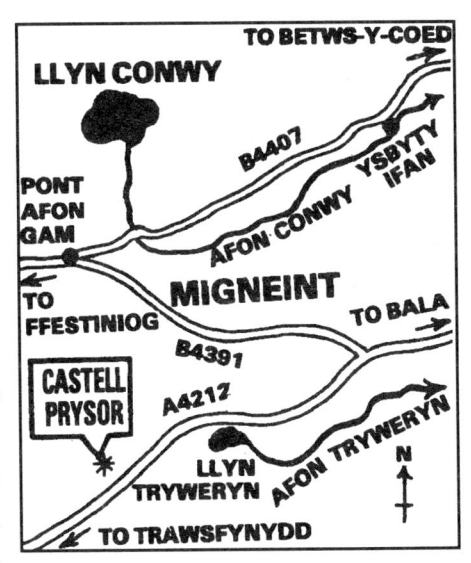

Where Prysor lies

Although badly ruined, at least ten courses of stonework, over six feet high, still stand. Large blocks of dressed stone could be identified, with smaller pieces placed to form a level surface for the next course of blocks to be laid. There was no sign of mortar on the facing of the wall, but in many places burrowing animals had cleaned out pieces of mortar and sea shells from the wall cavity spaces further in, and deposited them outside the burrows. This suggests that the wall was originally faced or revetted with mortared blocks. No evidence of a tower or keep survives, so it could have been a timber structure. There is evidence of a courtyard or bailey adjoining the motte to the north.

This type of castle was introduced into Britain by the Normans, and continued to be built in Wales well into the 13th century. The use of a natural hill or outcrop which was easy to defend, and strengthening it with mortared stone, was a common technique in north Wales in the 12th and early 13th centuries.

Castell Prysor cannot be precisely dated but, apart from its plan and building method, there are a few other clues to its origin.

The only historical reference to the castle is a letter addressed from it by Edward I on July 1, 1284. Since then it has had no recorded history, although it may have continued in use as a stronghold in the later Middle Ages. A survey of the area in 1590 mentions a boundary 'along Sarn Prysor over against the castle of Prysor . . . to Dôl Haidd'. Traces of an old road (sarn) can be seen near the castle.

Masonry – with mortar (Castell Prysor)

25. BETRAYAL AND AMBUSH
RICHARD II's AMBUSH SITE (GR 884786)

Today the A55 Expressway runs smoothly along the foot of the limestone cliffs of Penmaenrhos between Llanddulas and Colwyn Bay. The modern road has been safely engineered just above the high-water mark and is protected against the sea by twenty-two thousand twisted H-shaped concrete pillars, called 'dolos units', which were cast at Llanddulas.

Before the modern road was built, the narrow ledge between the sheer cliff-face and the sea had always been a problem for travellers. A document from the reign of James I (1624) mentions the need to make a way both 'above and below Penmaen for a coach lest the weather be foul, so that if they may not take one way they may be sure of the other'. But the cliffs continued to deter travelling until the end of the 18th century: 'It is so formidably narrow and unprotected that few people dare trust themselves or their horses upon it.'

At this time, Dr Johnson said that 'to spare the horrors of Penmaenrhos, we sent the coach over the road cross the mountain with Mrs Thrale . . . I, with Mr Thrale, walked along the edge where the path is very narrow and much encumbered by little loose stones which had fallen down since we passed before.' Two years later, in 1776, Cradock claimed that 'it was by far the worst part of the road between Holyhead and Chester.'

In the Middle Ages, this perilous track along the foot of Penmaenrhos was the scene of a famous ambush. An interesting possible link with this event was the finding, in 1894, of a gold half-noble coin of Richard II in a garden at Llanfairfechan. The coin was in good condition and showed the King aboard a sailing ship. On the reverse side, the inscription read 'Lord, rebuke me not in thine anger.' This text from the Bible was intended to discourage the crime of clipping coins.

How this fine coin came to be lost near Llanfairfechan, probably on an old track on the slopes of Garreg Fawr, is a

'Dolos' Units at the site of Richard II's ambush near Llanddulas

mystery. It may, however, be linked with the fact that Richard II and a small party were returning on horseback from Ireland and would have passed this spot. In the summer of 1399 they had landed at Milford Haven and were on their way to Conwy castle. The King's rival, Henry Bolingbroke, had been in exile, but had returned and been joined by many nobles. He was awaiting the king at Chester. Bolingbroke sent the Earl of Northumberland to Conwy and by swearing on holy relics on the altar of Conwy Castle garrison chapel, he persuaded Richard II to follow him to Rhuddlan.

Northumberland convinced Richard that Bolingbroke would settle their dispute peacefully, but the Earl returned in advance of the King and laid an ambush at Penmaenrhos. According to a contemporary record the King crossed Afon Conwy and 'rode for four miles until he came to the road where he saw the ambush, and knowing he was betrayed by the Earl of Northumberland'.

With the sea on one side and the cliffs on the other, and with

Gold Half Noble (Richard II)

only twenty-four men, he was reluctantly persuaded to continue to Rhuddlan castle for dinner and then on to Fflint castle for the night. The doomed king heard mass there on 22 August, 1399 and was then captured and taken to Pontefract Castle.

The ambush had been carefully sprung in the hollow on the eastern side of the cliffs, near the entrance to the present railway tunnel. It was the perfect site for an ambush, but is difficult to imagine it today with the Express-way sweeping along the foot of the cliffs.

26. FORT OVER THE VOLCANO
CASTELL DOLWYDDELAN (GR 722523)

In the 13th century, Dolwyddelan was one of a series being built by Llewelyn Fawr to consolidate his position in north Wales. There had been an earlier castle at Dolwyddelan, now badly ruined on its wooded hill near the river. It is referred to on the Ordnance Survey map as 'Tomen Castell'.

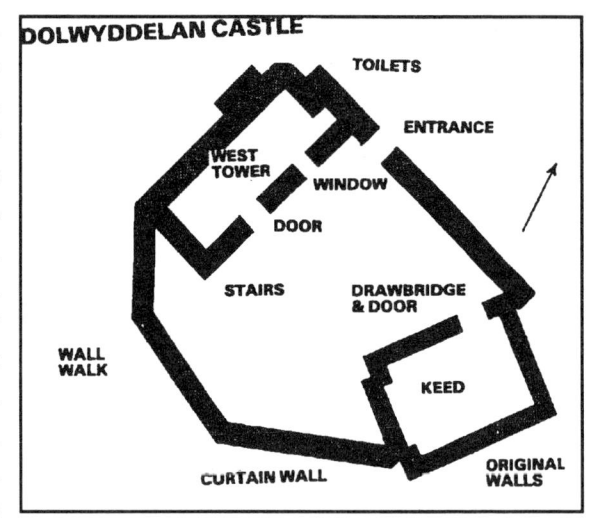

The builders of the new castle determined on a better site on a precipitous rocky crag with just enough room for a two-storied keep, a small courtyard and the west tower. The crag itself consisted of an ash that erupted from a volcano near Snowdon. It provided the perfect foundation for a tall building, but probably made the sinking of a well impossible for none has ever been found and it is supposed that the water supply may have been a pool or stream outside the walls of the castle.

The crag provided a very durable building stone that has withstood centuries of weathering, but that was not easy to work. It was laid irregularly with larger blocks roughly dressed on one face, which was then placed on the outside wall to give a smooth appearance. Even so, the castle walls are chiefly made of this uncoursed rubble of ash, with the spaces in-between filled with small pieces of slate. The blocks were embedded in mortar made of lime, with sand and pebbles from the nearby

Afon Lledr. The mortar has been washed out in places by the rain and redeposited as stalactites on the stonework. No single quarry was needed because practically all the masonry is of local rock dug from the crags and outcrops around the castle. Vast quantities of stone were needed to construct the thick walls, which are penetrated by an inside staircase and wall passages that visitors can still see.

Castell Dolwyddelan

Apart from the volcanic ash, the masons found use for the black slates of Dolwyddelan, and may have opened up what is now called Chwarel Ddu (black quarry), which lies near the castle and is filled in by a deep pool. The quarry may have been started on a small scale in the 13th century, but did not develop fully until the early 19th century. The slate was especially used for the doorways and windows; by looking carefully at the arches, one can almost imagine the stone mason choosing from a nearby pile the fine pieces of slate to place neatly in the arch. However, for the keystone in the arch he would select a wedge-shaped piece of volcanic ash. Slate was also used in steps and in lintels where a dressed stone was needed.

The only non-local rock is found in the south window and near the base of the doorway in the west tower, where a freestone was used which could be cut easily to give a moulded corner. This fine-grained sandstone is white or red in colour and is also found in Conwy Castle; but its exact outcrop source is unknown.

The keep and tower had wooden floors and beam holes in the stonework can still be clearly seen. A third storey was added to the keep in the late 15th century, but the builders used the same stone although the 'join' with the medieval castle is visible. The battlements were added in the late 19th century and in one place a neatly chiselled incsription reads 'Wilson, Conway, 1870'. The keep also retains the putlog holes where the medieval masons placed logs to support a scaffolding for building. At the top of the keep there is a neat series of slate drainage 'pipes' which drained the flat roof and a visitor once found pieces of lead in the courtyard which may have been from the old roof.

Unlike Conwy Castle, there are no documents about its construction but the architect and masons were able to get all their material and resources from within 200 yards (180m) of this spectacular site.

27. A WELSH PRINCE'S TOWER OF STRENGTH
CASTELL DOLBADARN (GR 585598)

Castell Dolbadarn

Castell Dolbadarn stands on the main route from the Menai Straits to the upper reaches of the Conwy Valley. In its lifetime it defended the innermost fastness of Eryri. It was in the heart of Llywelyn Fawr's kingdom and was probably built by him during his long reign from 1208-1240.

The main feature is the round stone tower or keep which was probably built about 1220-1230 in imitation of similar towers built by the Normans in their main strongholds in central Wales, in Pembroke and in the Marches.

It is very impressive on its rock crag overlooking Llyn Peris and still stands 48 feet (15m) above the rock base and has only lost a little of its original height. The finest quality work is in the tower, which is made of mortared, dressed stone and was constructed by the best masons. The entrance to the first floor was up an external staircase, now restored, to a door that led into the main royal apartment. The doorway was sealed by an iron gate known as the portcullis.

Near the entrance winding stone steps, a newel staircase around a central column, led to the second storey and was adequately lit by windows. This upper floor was supported on thick wooden beams. It had four windows which gave stunning views of the Llanberis pass. A fireplace with a chimney rising vertically through the wall can be seen, although the back has crumbled through burning. Both mains floors had chambers that led to toilets in the thick walls.

Apart from the tower, the rest of the castle was an irregular crescent-shaped, walled enclosure now reduced to its foundations. The walls were built of dry stone, and were originally 8 feet (2.4m) high and included the buildings that were needed to provision and maintain a garrison.

The castle had a fairly short life because its strategic importance was lost by 1283, after Edward I had completed his invasion and conquest, and following the killing of Llywelyn ap Gruffudd. Edward built his castles on the coast and had no need or interest in the Welsh castles that lay further inland.

There are no records for the castle from the time before the English conquest. Leland however quoted a tradition from the time of Henry VIII, that Llywelyn ap Gruffudd held his brother Owain as a prisoner here for about twenty years. The castle was seized by Edward I towards the end of the War of Independence (1282-3) and a document dated May 1284 records the removal of timber from the castle to be used in the construction of the new castle at Caernarfon. This timber was probably taken from the roof of the main tower, but the castle survived as a royal manor house and was eventually granted by Charles I to Sir Thomas Williams in 1627.

It would have been a formidable castle. The curtain wall around the courtyard would have given covering fire in all directions from its high crag. It is a worthy monument to the skills of the masons using the local stone, which included slate and volcanic ash.

It has been romantically depicted by numerous artists and is still a vivid reminder of days when the dream for freedom was still a tangible reality.

28. A ROUGH RIDE FOR ROYALTY
CASTELL FOELAS (GR 870523)

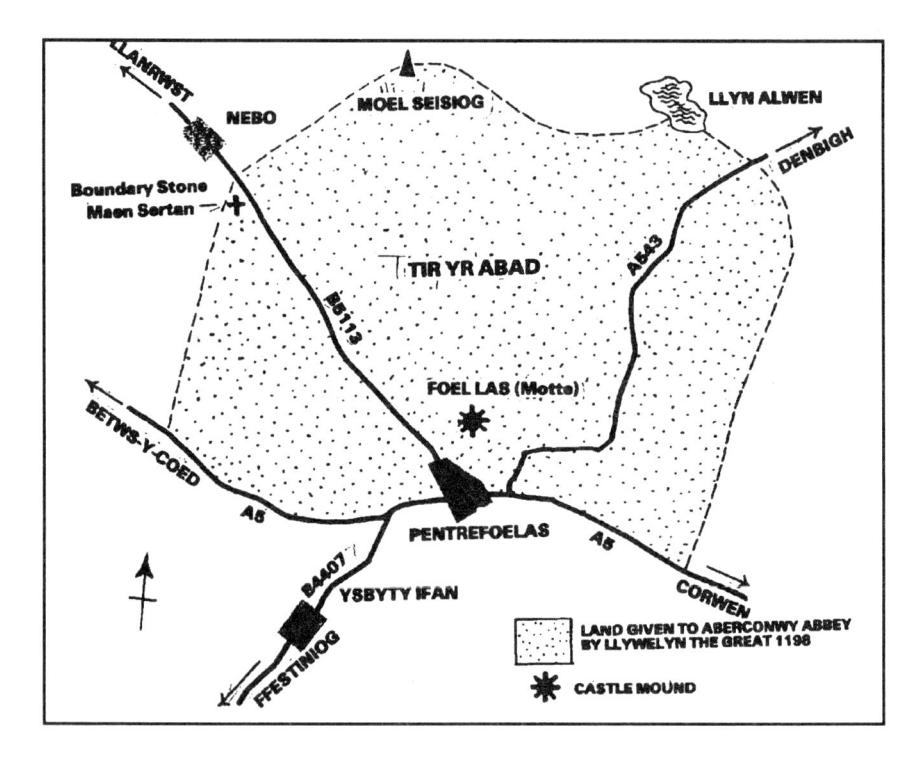

The name 'Foelas' appears in a document written at the end of the twelfth century, referring to a motte or castle mound half a mile (800m) north of the present village. It stands 30 feet (9m) above Nant-y-foel, a stream that supplied water to a surrounding moat, which can still be seen below the grass-covered hill.

In Norman times these mottes were built near streams using available pebbles and boulders. Sometimes they merely raised the level of an existing natural mound. Here, the stream has undercut part of the mound and has exposed a wall that was part of the original structure. There is no mortar in the wall, the blocks are irregular and a thick overlying turf layer suggests

Foelas – the castle mound (motte) at Pentrefoelas

that the wall is medieval and in fairly good condition after eight centuries of weathering.

In its day the motte would have held a wooden keep or tower and a defensive stockade. There were traces of a building on top of the mound reported in 1852. Records also show that there was a medieval township near the site of the present village.

This spot controlled the main route from England over the Berwyn range into Dyffryn Conwy. Indeed King Henry II used this route and Owain Gwynedd responded by building the castle at Foelas in 1164.

Thirty years later Llywelyn ap Iorwerth (Fawr) succeeded Owain, his grandfather. He replaced his uncle Dafydd from the area to the east across Hiraethog, known as Gwynedd is Conwy. A poem of this period names the strongholds which Llywelyn had to capture before he gained mastery over this part of north Wales, and they included Dinbych (Denbigh), Gronant and Foelas. The latter was seen as a threat; and Llywelyn sacked the castle, burnt it down and removed the garrison.

Llywelyn went on to strengthen his ties with the abbey at Aberconwy, at a spot around where the church of Conwy now stands. He drew up a charter to confirm the rights of the Cistertian monks in 1198 and gave grants of land in various parts of Gwynedd. This included a grant of land at Foelas to be used for sheep rearing and the grange and land became known as Tir yr Abad (land of the abbot).

The grange at Foelas survived until 1536 when Henry VIII dissolved the monasteries throughout Britain. Pentrefoelas became part of the parish of Llannefydd which was over 15 miles (24km) away across trackless moorland. The parishioners attended services at nearby Ysbyty Ifan but the banns of marriage had to be called at distant Llannefydd until 1766, when the Wynnes of Foelas built a church at Pentrefoelas.

29. STONE LETTERS THAT MATCH EARLY MANUSCRIPTS
LEVELINUS STONE – PENTREFOELAS
(GR 869522)

A tall inscribed stone pillar stood at a 'green gate' leading from what is now the A5 at Pentrefoelas to Hen Foelas (old hall) until 1790, It was then moved a short distance and was found, in 1912, standing in a small clearing in the wood near Castell Foelas.

It stands 8 feet (2.4m) high and 2 feet (60cm) broad with both upper and lower case letters inscribed on the stone. These had been copied in 1760, but the letters can still be seen, even after centuries of weathering. The stone was moved from its open-air site to the National Museum in Cardiff in 1940 and the lichens and mosses were cleared away. But weathered cracks in the stone make parts of the writing difficult to interpret.

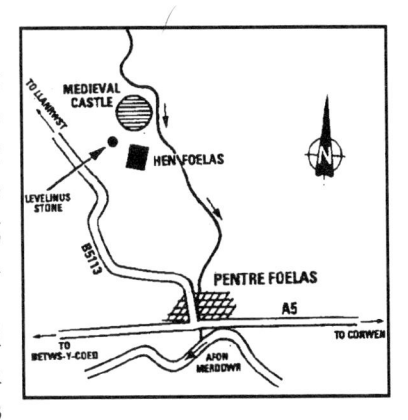

This stone has been puzzling historians for over four centuries, for it was first mentioned in 1586. Having been erected in the early years of the 13th century, it became covered in moss and lichen. The main damage, however, was done by rain and frost that penetrated the surface of the stone and disfigured some of the lettering. However, most of the letters are legible and are a mixture of Welsh and Latin. The most obvious word that can be picked out is 'Levelinus' and it has become known as the 'Levelinus Stone'. Its importance as a national monument is indicated by the fact that it is now on display in Cardiff.

The letters are exactly the same as those found in early 13th century manuscripts, thus suggesting that it was carved by monks or lay-brothers from the abbey at Aberconwy, who were also responsible for putting up the stone to commemorate their patron, Llywelyn ap Iorwerth (Fawr).

The choice of site is significant for it was near the medieval castle, on land that was given to the monastery by Llywelyn Fawr. This may explain why it was erected – they were this time thanking their patron for his generosity in granting them land around Pentrefoelas, which became known as 'Tir yr Abad'.

The exact date when the stone was inscribed and erected is not known, but it was probably shortly after the land was granted in the Charter of Aberconwy of 1189. The work on the stone must have been completed after 1198 when Llywelyn came to use the title Tywysog Gogledd Cymru (Prince of North Wales) and before 1230, from when he used the title Tywysog Aberffraw ac Arglwydd Eryri (Prince of Aberffraw and Lord of Snowdonia). Further evidence to support this supposition is that the letters are almost exactly the same as the lettering used in two famous Black Books (Llyfrau Duon), which were written about 1200.

The stones' message is recorded in verse, and this has given rise to different views and meanings. One interpretation is that it is dedicated to 'Llywelyn, Prince of North Wales, who raised me (the stone) up with the strength of his arm'. Another takes the view however that it is a play on the word 'Llywelyn', and that it reads: 'Thy name, Llywelyn, is from Llew (Lion) and from might of arm, O Levelinus, Prince of North Wales'.

It was aimed at Welshmen who had some Latin, the language of the Law and the Church at that time. There are three lines of verse, and the last lines is not in doubt, for it reads:
'Leveline, Princeps: Norh Vallie'.
'Llywelyn: Prince of North Wales.'
This final line preserves a bit of the medieval past for it puts us in direct contact with Llywelyn ap Iorwerth, who dominated Welsh politics in the first three decades of the 13th century.

30. MEDIEVAL RELICS OF THE GREAT ELIZABETHAN AGE
COED-Y-FFYNNON – PENMACHNO (GR 804531)

Coed-y-Ffynnon near Penmachno

An attractive feature of Cwm Machno are the fine 16th-17th century houses where the small landowners lived in modest comfort with domestic servants and farm workers. The houses date back to the settled times following the end of the Wars of the Roses in the 16th century. They still show some of the features of the medieval style of building in Eryri.

However, the open hall had been replaced by a second storey with a spiral staircase leading up from the side of the kitchen fireplace to private bedrooms. The houses were built of local stone which was usually volcanic boulders and slate rubble with some massive blocks over four feet long. The thick walls kept out the winter gales and were regularly whitewashed to give a striking appearance. Small windows and low oak beams are a feature and the small doorways with porches added further protection against the weather.

Inside the house, planks of wood were used to partition the rooms, the doors had wooden latches, and oak chests were used to store oatmeal. Fresh spring water was drawn from the stone-lined well across the yard. Plenty of timber was available from the scrub oakwood, the birch and the beech trees around the house.

Near the house stood a large stone barn with arrow-slit ventilation holes. It was a substantial building because the farm was self-supporting and had to store ample supplies of corn for the family needs, as well as animal fodder and seed corn for the following season.

Cwm Machno has more than its fair share of these Elizabethan and Jacobean houses, and a superb example is Coed-y-Ffynnon on the hill above the woollen mill near Penmachno. As its name suggests, referring to woods and a well, it had timber supplies and fresh water. The fields stretched down to the river, and the fishing rights on Pwll yr Afanc *(Beaver Pool)* near Betws-y-coed and the salmon leap on Afon Lledr belonged to the family.

The fields below the house are now planted with trees but once held, according to tradition, a medieval chapel or chantry where prayers were sung to departed souls. The slope is still shown as 'Buarth Tan yr Eglwys' on the Ordnance Survey maps, and remains of the foundations may still exist.

Isolation is very much a modern concept, created by a consumer society's constant need for amenities. Country communities of old were largely self sufficient and, far from everywhere as this place seems, this was not an isolated spot. Medieval (and probably much older) tracks ran uphill to Fedw Deg which was another old house, and past Tŷ Nant to Dolwyddelan.

The old part of the house dates from the 16th century, with some original features remaining such as a small window on the south side and the porch with its arched doorway, which could be a relic from the old chantry. The square chimneys with the horizontal plate near the top is another tell-tale sign of its age.

Inside one noticeable feature is the Coat of Arms, which is a fine plaster shield in relief with six separate 'pictures'. These six quarters show lions, chevrons with fleur-de-lis and a Saracen's head. The four lions were the crest of the Welsh princes and the head on the shield is derived from the Arms of Ednyfed Fychan, who was marshall to Llywelyn the Great.

In the 16th century, this display of a Coat of Arms revived the old custom which originated in the castles of the Middle Ages. Such shields were a feature in the great hall above the large fireplaces of the medieval castles.

There are eighteen houses in Dyffryn Conwy, that were built in the 16th-17th centuries, which have fine plasterwork exhibiting the family's Coat of Arms. Some of these houses also have date-stones that indicate when they were built. Hafod Dwyryd near Penmachno has a date-stone of 1678. Some were occupied by well-known local families, such as the Lloyds of Dylasau. Little is known about daily domestic life, but the houses have fortunately survived as a splendid record of their age.

31. PILGRIMS' HALT AND OUTLAWS' SANCTUARY
CHURCH – YSBYTY IFAN (GR 844489)

The splendid village of Ysbyty Ifan was once given a Latin name - Hospitium Johannis. It is peacefully tucked away in a green hollow in the upper reaches of Afon Conwy. The name derives from 'St John's Hospital', which recalls a colourful medieval history. The Knights of St John were a crusading order with the highest ideals of service and they set up a church and hospice in Jerusalem after the Holy Places had been taken from the Moslems during the Crusades.

Effigies in Ysbyty Ifan Church

In return for their efforts they were rewarded with land and revenue in western Europe, including Wales. In 1190, in the days of Llywelyn ap Iorwerth (Fawr), they were given land to build a church and hospice at Ysbyty Ifan. The spot was then on a busy route from Chester and Rhuthun to Cerrigydrudion and the ford at Pont Saint. The route continued to Ynys Enlli (Bardsey), the island of 20,000 saints and a centre of pilgrimage. Ysbyty Ifan was a suitable halt.

In 1220 Llywelyn gave more land and money from various churches and manors to the order of St John but following the conquest by Edward I, the hospice fell into neglect as law and order broke down. However, it retained its right of sanctuary and was outside the rule of the King's Law. Lawbreakers settled around Ysbyty Ifan and used it as a base for raids. Their rule of terror and pillage ran from Conwy to Bala and Dinbych.

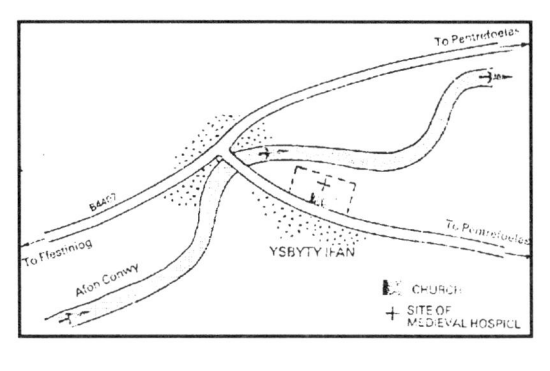

Sir John Wynn of Gwydir recalled that his ancestor Maredudd ap Ieuan bought the castle at Dolwyddelan, which itself had been a robber's stronghold in the 15th century. He gradually reduced the power of the criminals in the Nant Conwy area. From his newly-built house he needed twenty 'minders' to accompany him to Dolwyddelan church'. He left guards at his house and posted a watchman on a high rock at Carreg y Big to warn of possible ambush. But through the efforts of Maredudd ap Ieuan and others, a form of rule had been restored in Nant Conwy by the early 16th century and the Kings' Court was held here in 1529.

This local 'dynasty' is now represented by three alabaster effigies in the church. Rhys ap Maredudd led a troop of men from the area in support of Henry Tudor at the Battle of Bosworth in 1485. By his side is Lowri, his wife, dressed in contemporary costume. The third effigy is that of Robert ap Rhys their son who became chaplain to Cardinal Wolsey.

The Vaughans flourished as county squires in Nant Conwy (the higher regions of Dyffryn Conwy). They had their own chapel at Ysbyty Ifan and alms-houses were built with money from Katherine Vaughan, who died in 1700. Their fine house at Pant Glas stood until 1795 when the roof fell in. The remains of the windows and mantlepieces however were still existing in outbuildings of nearby farms into the 19th century. When the old church was demolished in 1858, portions of freestone tombs and window jambs belonging to a still earlier church were found in the walls, but no trace of the hospice.

The plaque on the church gate recently set up by the Hospitallers refers to the Hospice as being within the precincts of the church and is a valuable recognition of its historic importance.

32. MAY DAY EXODUS TO THE HUTS IN THE HILLS
HAFOTAI – ABERGWYNGREGIN (GR 667704)

From the Bronze Age until at least the 17th century, many farmers had two houses if they farmed in the uplands of Wales. The hendre (winter residence) was in the valley and the hafod or hafoty (summer house) was in the hills. The map shows that over thirty hafotai still exist as place names in Dyffryn Conwy alone.

None of the earliest hafotai have survived, probably because they would have been rather flimsy structures. Their replacements, however, were huts with dry-stone walls, and ruins of these long huts can be seen on the slopes of Pen-y-castell, west of Dolgarrog, and in the valley below Rhaeadr Fawr (Aber Falls).

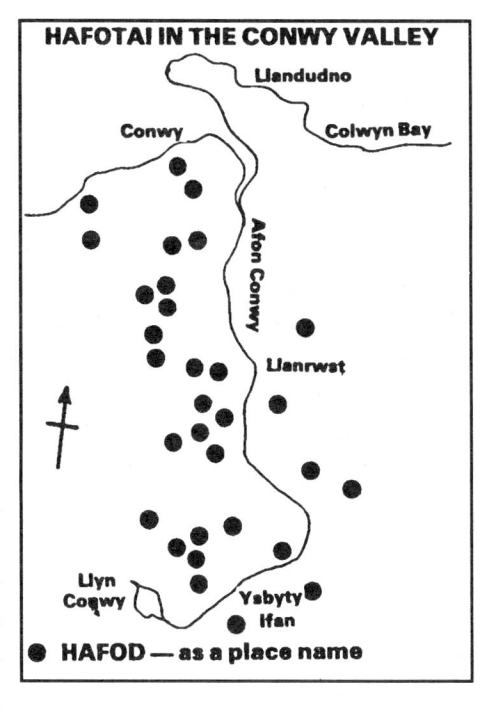

The farmer and his family moved the livestock from the lower lands and lived with them in the hills from early May until late September. The traditional day for moving up was Calan Mai *(May Day)*, after oats had been sown near the hendre. They spent their time with the rest of the family cutting moorland hay, herding and milking cattle, and making cheese and butter. Mountain butter was considered sweeter than butter made in the valley.

The way of life was vividly reported by Thomas Pennant in

1773 when he described visiting a hafod in the mountains west of Capel Curig.

'Their houses consist of a long, low room with a hole at one end to let out the smoke from the fire. Their furniture is very simple; stones for stools and beds of hay. During the summer the men pass their time in harvest or tending their herds while the women are engaged in making butter and cheese. Their diet is very plain, consisting of butter, cheese and oat bread (bara ceirch), and they drink whey. They are people of good understanding, wary and circumspect. Usually they are tall, thin and of strong constitution from their way of living.'

There is a fine example of a group of long hut hafotai about 600 yards (550m) north of Rhaeadr Fawr at the side of the path to the Aber Falls. The nine huts were excavated in the 1950's, and one was considered to be of medieval origin. There is indeed a record of cattle herding in Aber in 1303, and hafotai were actually named in the valley as Meuryn and Nant. The door of this hut faced south, away from the prevailing winds. The other huts were built and occupied in the 18th century. Some had paved floors and were used as a dairy and for drying flax. The huts were roughly furnished with beds of hay and heather and utensils were made of wood. Skin bags were used to store water. Most such materials were perishable, which may explain why the excavation in 1950 only yielded pottery. There were jug fragments of brown glazed pottery made in Buckley in the late 18th century.

A single find of a pot of black vitrified ware suggested that the hafotai had fallen into disuse in the early years of the 19th century, which may have been due to the spread of sheep farming at the expense of cattle.

33. IRONMAN TAMED A VALLEY'S RIFF-RAFF
MAREDUDD AP IEUAN – DOLWYDDELAN (GR 742508)

Nant Conwy's wooded valleys had long been notorious when Maredudd ap Ieuan sought refuge at Castell Dolwyddelan in 1488. Rogues were attracted to the area because of the sanctuary at the hospice of St John's at Ysbyty Ifan. And at the end of the Wars of the Roses, many soldiers and retainers were quite readily drawn into a life of lawlessness.

According to Sir John Wynne in his History of the Gwydir Family, Maredudd ap Ieuan was escaping the threat of murder at the hands of his relatives at the ancestral home at Penmorfa near Criccieth. The castle at Dolwyddelan provided a secure base on its high crag above Dyffryn Lledr and within sight of the old 12th century church below.

Carreg Alltrem near Dolwyddelan

Maredudd built an extra floor to the castle tower, keeping the medieval style of windows and stone work and using the local rock-black Dolwyddelan slate and volcanic ash. Just below the flat roof level he built a line of slate corbels so that water could drain clear of the castle wall.

He had not been long at the castle before he built a new house at Penamnen across the valley, and in a spate of rebuilding removed the old church from the wooded hill where it had stood since the twelfth century.

He rebuilt the church on a new site about 300 yards (270m) to the east, in a more open position on the flat floor of Dyffryn Lledr. The new church, Tŷ Penamnen and the castle gave him a secure power base in the area. Twelve years after building the church, he installed a glass window with fragments of stained glass in the east wall of the chancel, and until the last century the date of the window (1512) was recorded on the nearby wall. The window is still intact and there is a brass plaque to commemorate Maredudd on the north wall of the church at Dolwyddelan.

When he went to church from his new house at Penamnen, he took with him twenty 'minders' who were stout archers, and a watchman was left on top of Carreg Alltrem, opposite the house with a perfect view of the castle and the new church. He acquired cottages as they became empty in the surrounding area and gave their tenancy to 'tall and able men'. Through this action he was able to build a formidable force of one hundred and forty archers who were ready to assemble whenever the sound of the bugle was heard from the castle. According to Sir John Wynne's account, they had a uniform of a 'jacket or armoured coat, a steel cap, a dagger and bow and arrows'. With this force he was able to curb the activity of thieves and by the time of his death in 1525 had secured a good measure of law and order in the area. The King's Court was held for the first time in Nant Conwy in 1525.

Revisiting Dolwyddelan today, we can still see the buildings which vividly recall the early years of the sixteenth century. The castle and church still survive almost in the same condition but there is no trace of the old church at Bryn-y-Bedd, which he considered too risky to attend because of its concealed position in a 'thicket'. All that remains of the house that he built at

Maredudd ap Ieuan's house in Cwm Penamnen

Penamnen is solid masonry up to 6 feet (1.8m) high on the roadside in the present-day forest. It is now a ruin but the roof was intact earlier in the 20th century. From the front door, a gap in the forest gives a sensational view of Carreg Alltrem, which was the look-out point.

34. PLAS IOLYN NEAR PENTREFOELAS
PLAS IOLYN (GR 881503)

Sixteenth Century (1572) Barn at Plas Iolyn

The oldest visible structure at Plas Iolyn is a 12 foot (3.6m) square tower of large dry stone blocks, with one wall cut into the edge of a rock-face and the lower chamber excavated into the outcrop itself. This basement or cellar has a square-headed, deeply-splayed window which gave some restricted light to this dark room. The entrance was through a narrow arched doorway that resembled a church door and led into a courtyard.

The first-floor room above was the main living room, with a fireplace. A dressed stone with a moulded corner has survived as the jamb of a fireplace. Above this there was a second floor, which is now almost completely ruined and offers no further clues to the use and function of the tower. It was obviously a basic defensive building, and was almost certainly the first building on this site. Immediately outside the arched door entrance there is the remains of a 35 foot (11m) deep, circular well drilled through solid rock, which is a common feature of all the early structures here. The well may be contemporary with the tower because it has a strong resemblance to the wells found in medieval castles, with its 5 foot (1.5m) diameter and a lining of stone blocks. The well continued in use until the 1930's when it was used in the process of churning butter. It then became overgrown and was capped in 1957.

The tower and the well on this rock crag would have provided a perfect site for a medieval stronghold. There is documentary evidence that Ifan ap Rhys, Lord of the area known as Trebrys, gave land to the Knight Hospitallers to build a hospice at Ysbyty Ifan in 1180. The area also became important in the early 13th century with the grant of sheep pasture to the Cistercian monastery at Aberconwy. The construction of small stone castles at such strategic points was a feature of the period, so there is a possibility that the tower at Plas Iolyn can be traced to this period (1180-1220). A defensive site with a clean-water supply would be a focus of settlement for the local leader. It may have survived for over two centuries in the hands of the same family. In 1450 Maredudd ap Tudur, a direct descendant of Ifan ap Rhys, was steward of land in Hiraethog belonging to the abbey of Aberconwy, as well as lands belonging to the knights of St John at nearby Ysbyty Ifan.

The main chapter began with the career of Maredudd's son, Rhys ap Maredudd, who fought at Bosworth Field in 1485 with a regiment of Welsh Highland troops. He carried Henry Tudor's banner and was rewarded with land including large tracts in Trebrys, around the Tower at Plas Iolyn. Tudor Penllyn, a poet who died in 1490, said that Rhys Fawr built a house of wood on a foundation of stones that giants could not move but, unfortunately, he does not say where this was built. It is likely that it was the original Plas Iolyn that replaced the old tower which was too cramped for his large family of eleven sons and daughters. The tower had also possibly outlived its usefulness as a defensive site.

Building new houses on more open and spacious sites was a common development in the more peaceful parts of north Wales in this period. Only the foundations of the house that Rhys built at this time may have survived however, because his son Rhobert inherited the old home which he rebuilt in accordance with his wealth and status. Sir Rhobert ap Rhys was chaplain and cross-bearer to Cardinal Wolsey and acquired leases on monastic lands, as well as land owned by the Knights Hospitallers at Ysbyty Ifan in 1506. He was accused of maintaining his own body of soldiers and of imprisoning people in St John's hold at Ysbyty Ifan. He amassed a great fortune and build a new house at Plas Iolyn. It had, according to a contemporary account, large chimneys, a cross-chamber, a round cellar for storing wine, and was 'a house of stone up to the roof', a lime-washed mansion. It is probable that it was built on the foundations of his father's old house, next to the medieval tower. It is highly likely that Rhobert built the tithe barn in this period (up to 1530) against the side wall of the derelict tower, which it partly enclosed. A barn was essential to collect and store corn brought in from tithes. The barn was strongly constructed of large rough blocks of stone but with dressed stone at the corners; some chamfered corner stones (quoins) and neat arrow-slit ventilation slits show careful construction methods. Building stone and methods of construction are in sharp contrast to the adjoining medieval tower and it is likely that the tithe barn was built in the period 1500-1530 when Rhobert was building his mansion at Plas Iolyn.

After Rhobert's death in 1534 the house passed to his eldest son Dafydd but it was a younger son, Elis Prys (also known as Y Doctor Coch), who eventually settled here. In 1560 he obtained a grant from Queen Elizabeth of the manor and lands of Ysbyty Ifan on the Denbighshire side known as 'Tir Ifan'. A poem written in 1572-3 states that Elis Prys had renewed the walls and house of his father and went on to praise the finely-built walls, large wine cellars, glass windows, the dog-leg staircase and the hall that was as large as that of a palace.

This final phase (1560-72) was also matched by the construction of another barn needed to store the corn that tithes brought in from parishes under his control. At one time he had charge of parishes at Llandrillo-yn-Rhos, Llanuwchllyn, Llangar as well as Ysbyty Ifan and Penmachno. On a collar beam in the roof, the date 1572 is clearly inscribed in bas relief and is probably a good clue not only to the date of the barn but also the house itself. Elis Prys was very wealthy at this time and was an agent of the Earl of Leicester and able to extort taxes and dues.

35. THE STATUS SYMBOLS OF AN AGE OF CONQUESTS
GILER (GR 884499)

Giler near Pentrefoelas

Four old mansions lie close together near Pentrefoelas on the old drovers' road, these being Foelas, Cerniogau, Plas Iolyn and Giler.

Giler was built about 1600, at a time when the single hall with unglazed windows and an open hearth in the centre of the floor, was being replaced by a newer design. The old medieval hall-houses open to the rafters were full of smoke and gave little privacy and no comfort for the occupants. The 'new' houses had two storeys with a spiral staircase in the thick walls next to the fireplace and, for added luxury, glazed windows.

A large number of fine massive chimneys displayed the owner's wealth and the gentry bequeathed their glass windows

Giler (Gatehouse)

in their wills. Glass was scarce in the 16th century and up to 1600 domestic windows were replicas of church windows, with two tall lights and decoration above. Oak floors and oak-panelled walls gave a warm glow to the fire-lit interior rooms. and oak cupboards and settles added to the comfort. They were fond of displaying a coat of arms which were designed as a plaster panel above the fireplace.

Giler was built in this fashion about 1600 by Prys Wynn and, in 1623, was extended by his son Thomas ap Prys Wynn. He also built a fine gatehouse which stood at the bottom of a cobbled path and was the official entrance to a walled courtyard in front of the house. The initials TPW in quartz pebbles are still visible in the path, and his initials and a 1623 date stone appears over the arched gatehouse. The gatehouse is in excellent condition for it was built as a status symbol, just before Thomas was appointed High Sheriff of Denbighshire.

It guarded the entrance to a large walled courtyard which

was full of flowers, bushes, herbs and, perhaps, cages of songbirds. The nail-studded oak door leads into an arched passageway above which is the guardroom. An outside staircase led to this small room which had a plaster panel above the fireplace. The coat of arms shows a rose, a lion, a griffin and three heads which was the coat of arms of Thomas ap Prys Wynn. The house, gatehouse and walled courtyard have changed little over almost 400 years.

The thick walls are made of rubble of split volcanic rocks and coarse grit stone found locally and lying on uneven outcrops of hard rock. The neat stone-lined mullioned windows and the arched porch with nail-studded door retain the original character.

Although the house has been adapted over the years, with a modern slate roof and new chimneys, Giler is still substantially the same as it was in the days of Shakespeare and gives a strong sense of continuous history in these bleak hills above Pentrefoelas

36. FARMER'S OLD BARN SAVED FOR A MUSEUM
CRUCK BARN AT HENDRE WEN (GR 805588)

Cruck Barn now in St Fagan's, Cardiff

Hendre Wen is a farm lying two miles south of Llanrwst at the end of a farm track from the A470. It is the only place in Dyffryn Conwy to have contributed a valuable building to the National Folk Museum at St Fagan's, Cardiff.

On the farm road, but a good distance from the farm itself, there was an old barn that was derelict by 1972, but which attracted the attention of the museum because it was a fine example of a cruck barn.

The simplest method of building in medieval times was to find timber in which the trunk and a thick branch could be cut and split to form the home's side and roof frame. These shaped pieces were called 'crucks' and by the 16th century were a tried and tested method of building barns in the Midlands of England and in east Wales. Hendre Wen was the most westerly out-post of this style, which was not used in Eryri because stone was plentiful.

Hendre Wen barn before removal: view from the south

But, in the 16th century, according to Sir John Wynn of Gwydir, Dyffryn Conwy had plenty of trees. Three large crucks were cut and raised to form the basic frame of the barn. They rested on padstones within the walls which were made of massive boulders left behind by glaciers and along the river banks. When the crucks were raised to roof-top height, they were strengthened by cross-beams. The rest of the building was made of dry stone walls forming the base and a gable end, with a timber frame and weather board.

The three crucks separated four bays or rooms with partitions of wattle and daub. A sturdy roof of rough-cut slate gave a weather-proof barn for storing oats, straw, a loft for threshed straw, a threshing floor and a space for cattle with a tell-tale soakaway. The crucks were trimmed smooth on one-side for pegging the cross beams and the outside walls were rendered in mud to fill in between the dry stones.

The history of the barn has unfortunately been complicated by the fact that it was re-built in 1800 using the original materials. A dish of Buckley pottery found in the dismantling of the barn in 1972 supports this date for rebuilding.

The museum at St Fagan's got permission to remove the barn by 1972. The stones and slates were carefully numbered and re-set near Cardiff. The biggest task was raising the one-ton crucks into position for they were 25 feet ((7.8m) high when lifted, and it needed twenty men using struts and ropes to raise them. They now form a superb feature and can be reliably dated to the 16th century.

All the building materials were local with oak from the valley, mud from the river bank, boulders from the river and slates from the hills near Trefriw. Over the years however, many of the roof slates had been lost and Dr Eurwyn William, who was in charge of the re-building appealed for local slate to re-roof the barn.

The barn now stands in the grounds at St Fagan's as a superb reminder of the building methods used in Dyffryn Conwy centuries ago.

37. TO THE RESCUE OF THE LOST TRAVELLER
JOHN OGILBY'S MAPS

The days when travellers struck out across the treacherous Traeth Lafan on their journey to Ynys Môn are illustrated in the work of a famous map-maker.

John Ogilby (1600-1676) surveyed and published a plan of London after the Great Fire of 1666. He became Charles II's 'geographic printer' and published road maps, which were made into a book called Britannia in 1675. These maps were the first of their kind and resembled present-day AA road-maps.

To make his maps, he walked all the main roads from London to various places in England and Wales, and with a wheel measured exact distances which were then recorded on the maps. He also added geographical information such as rivers, bridges, towns, castles as well as mountains and coastal features.

These were the earliest strip road-maps of England and Wales and were years ahead of their time; they became the model for map makers for the next hundred years. The maps look strangely modern with roads with enclosing hedges shown as black lines whereas dash lines show unenclosed roads. Unlike earlier maps which were based on impressions, these maps which were based on survey and measurement. He used 1760 yards (1636m) as the accepted length of a mile, long before it became the official 'statute' mile enacted by Parliament.

In the book the maps are shown as a scroll or strip from the bottom left-hand corner to the top of the page. The road from Chester to Holyhead takes one page with seven separate strips and is easy to read. One strip shows the road leaving Conwy along the edge of Morfa Conwy and along the foot of Penmaenbach and Penmaenmawr. It then struck out across Traeth Lafan, where a warning indicates that they should only be crossed at low water, to a point opposite Beaumaris where a short ferry operated.

The map also showed an alternative route to Bangor down the bottom of the Sychnant Pass and across the notorious Penmaenmawr which was to be used 'when ye tide is in'. The direct 'road' across Traeth Lafan shows the distances in miles from London, probably because only people living and working in the city could afford to buy it.

Map makers and publishers of guide books copied Ogilby's map for north Wales without alteration for most of the eighteenth century. Even so, in Ogilby's day, the Traeth Lafan crossing was losing its popularity, as is shown by the remarks in 1669 of Revd William Williams that the stretch of sand at low water from Penmaenmawr to Beaumaris was 'formerly the direct route to Ireland'. The road across the sand was very exposed and dangerous, the ferry could only be used at low tide which restricted its use to about four hours a day.

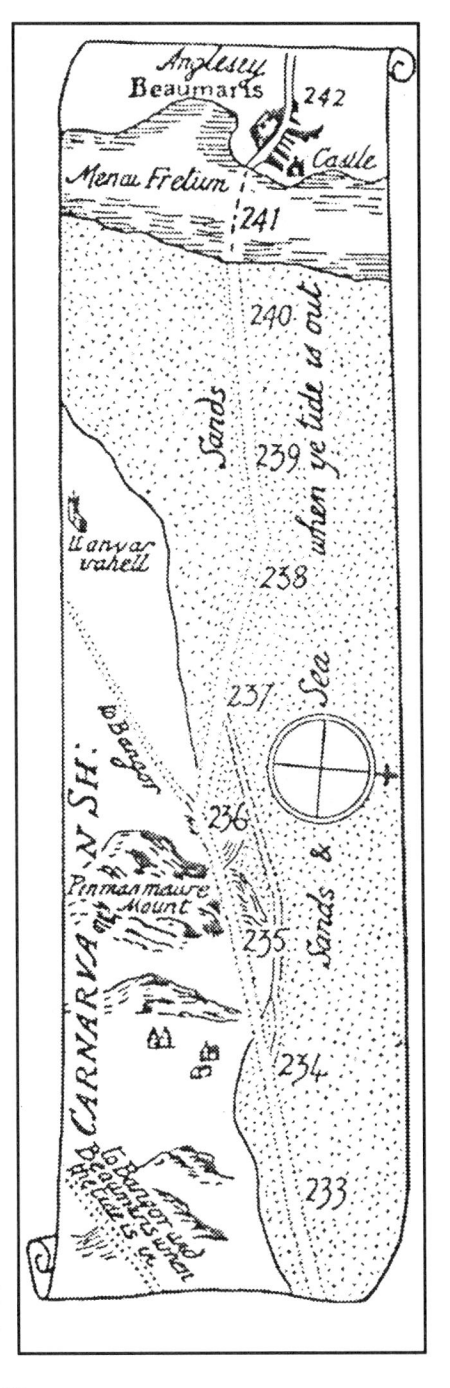

So when Ogilby's map was published the land route to Bangor was already replacing the Traeth Lafan route, for the ferryman at Porthaethwy (Menai Bridge) was granted a licence to build a house there in 1687. By the end of the seventeenth century, travellers to Ynys Môn preferred the longer route through Bangor. Travellers on horseback would have been equipped with warm cloaks and hip-length boots to cope with the weather, the rocky surfaces and the mud.

A great hazard on Traeth Lafan was fog. The church bell at Aber tolled during periods of fog to give direction to travellers caught out on the four-mile stretch.

38. ANCIENT HUTS BUILT UNDER MOONLIGHT . . .
TAI UNNOS

Tai-Un-Nos Cottage. Extremely rare - the name (Tai un nos) is still retained and the original dwelling still survives on the right attached to the later cottage. On the side of a deep valley.

The building of a tŷ unnos (a house built between sunset and dawn) on a waste corner or common land was an old custom in Wales. Such flimsy homes were built in large numbers in many parts of the country. They were single-storey houses and had a single living room separated from a bedroom by a wattle partition. In some cases, a low attic over the sleeping area was made for children, but they would have to roll out of bed.

Farm labourers often lived in the loft above the stables on the farm where they worked. When they married, they needed their own house. With the help of friends and relatives they would build a turf house on common land using a time-honoured tradition dating back to the laws of Hywel Dda. The chosen spot would probably be on the mountainside where rock, marsh and bracken discouraged farming. The main necessity was that the house had to be built during the course of one night and completed by sunrise.

The best time was a moonlit night in May or June, but the prospective owner would spend weeks beforehand secretly collecting supplies of flag-stones for the hearth, buttress poles, roof timbers, turf, brushwood and heather. These were placed near the site so that they did not need any long-distance carting. On the night chosen for the operation, the builders would make a rough stone wall, sometimes placed on an existing hedgebank. They would raise a simple timber roof, an under-thatch of brushwood, and finally place the overlapping turf sods. The house would be 'legal' provided smoke was issuing from the chimney before dawn, and the owner could also claim the land around the house as far as he could throw an axe from the door. He could at a later date build a turf wall around his boundary to confirm his ownership.

The house would not be designed for long-term occupation and many only lasted a few years. They would quickly lapse into decay after harsh winters and the owner would replace it with a permanent stone cottage, but keeping the original small, low shape that is still apparent today.

Little documentary evidence exists to say confidently that a present-day whitewashed cottage on a hillside is descended from the parent tŷ unnos. The simple houses were given descriptive names such as Tŷ Tywyrch (turf house), but were later renamed when stone replaced turf so that Tŷ Newydd (new house) became a common name in north Wales.

The period when they flourished was 1795-1810 during the Napoleonic Wars before Parliament had passed the Enclosure Acts to enclose the hill lands and establish ownership. Many houses were built at Llanddeiniolen and it is on record that in the first decade of the 19th century, seventeen new houses were built on waste land at Penmachno.

On the hill-slopes above Llanfairfechan squatters were producing plentiful crops of potatoes and even barley, so there must have been turf cottages on the slopes of Garreg Fawr, Dinas and Penmaenhead.

One of the few records of an actual cottage is mentioned in

Hugh Evans' book Cwm Eithin, in which he mentions a tŷ unnos named 'Bryn Bras' on the edge of Cerrigydrudion. It was built by Gabriel Parry who made a living by buying home-made woollen stockings on the local farms and then selling them in nearby fairs. He depended on the help of friends to build his turf house and was so poor that he didn't possess a spade, pickaxe or crowbar. Very few of these houses have survived in their original form but their replacement stone-built cottages still exist or have become ruins.

39. BURIAL SITE OF THE HOUNDED FRIENDS
QUAKERS (MEMORIAL – LLYN CELYN) (GR 876405)

Quaker Memorial Stone at the shoreline of Celyn Reservoir near Bala

A huge boulder stands near the dam across Llyn Celyn (reservoir), north of Bala, on a slate pavement by the roadside. It overlooks the lake, and its engraved metal plate that has been inscribed in both Welsh and English records the site of a Quaker burial ground. It reads:

'Under these waters and near this stone stood Hafod Fadog, a farmstead where in the 17th and 18th centuries Quakers met to worship. On the hill above the house was a space enclosed by a low stone wall where larger meetings were held. Beyond was a small burial ground. From the valley came many of the early Quakers who migrated to Pennsylvania, driven from their homes by persecution to seek freedom of worship in the New World.'

The hillside farm of Hafod Fadog stood there until 1959, when work on the reservoir was started. Everybody then living in the Cwm Tryweryn knew that a Quaker graveyard, known locally as Mynwent y Crynwyr, stood near the farm. It had an enclosing wall and was overgrown with bushes. An eye-witness could not remember whether any tombstones had survived until 1959. There was a strong local tradition that ancestors of

Abraham Lincoln had been buried there.

The Quakers (Society of Friends) were founded in 1652 by George Fox, encouraged by the freedom of religion granted by Cromwell. No formal religious organisation was needed, and most of their services were held in the open air, on farms or in meeting houses. But after 1660 their opposition to the payment of tithes and taking the oath of allegiance created a backlash of persecution. Despite this persecution, the Quaker movement took root in many parts of Meirionnydd, particularly around Bala, Dolgellau and on the west coast at Llwyngwril.

There are detailed records of individual Quakers being persecuted in Bala after 1660. They were charged with failure to attend church and refusing the oath of allegiance. At the Assizes in Bala, John ap Thomas who was a local Quaker was brought before the court. He lived on the hillside farm of Llaith Gwm, which still stands a few miles north of Bala. He was 'convinced' as a Quaker in 1672. After being charged, John was watched and it was reported that he had attended two Quaker meetings. He was fined £15 and lost a horse and two heifers to the unnamed informer, but continued to preach and eventually lost most of his livestock in fines. His health deteriorated and he fled to London, leaving his wife and eight children at home.

In London he negotiated with William Penn to buy land near Philadelphia in what later became Pennsylvania. His friend, Edward Jones went over to see the land and was impressed – rich soil, plenty of timber and water, and friendly Indians who brought venison to the door. The only problems were shortages of millstones, iron and particularly salt.

But John ap Thomas died in London in 1683 and was secretly returned to his birthplace to be buried on the Quaker burial plot at Hafod Fadog. The next farm was Ciltalgarth, which still stands today above the lake. Here lived a well-known Quaker, Hugh Roberts who later emigrated to Pennsylvania. He returned to visit his old home at Ciltalgarth in 1697 and was welcomed back by huge crowds.

40. CATTLE 'BARONS' WHO RODE THE WILD MOORLAND
DROVERS BRIDGE AT TAI-HIRION (GR 804398)

Tai-hirion (Drover's) Bridge near Arennig

One of the finest small bridges in North Wales lies on the bleak Migneint moors to the south-west of Ysbyty Ifan. It's built of roughly dressed local stone in the shape of a simple arch, on foundations of large boulders placed on each bank of the stream. The underside of the arch is smoothly finished and shows the skill and pride of the masons, who left no date or record of its origin.

There are relics of an old road with stone kerbs which leads to the grassed slabs which form the surface of the bridge today. There was no parapet on the bridge, and with a width of only just over 6 feet (1.2m), it would have been used as a pack-horse bridge over Afon Tai-hirion.

At the end of the 17th century, Edward Lhuyd recorded the

names of many bridges in North Wales, and mentioned this as Pont Rhyd y Porthmon located 1 mile (1.6km) from Tai Hirion, which is an old long-house.

The word 'porthmon' is Welsh for 'drover'. From Elizabethan times and possibly earlier, these hardy men used the old road across the Migneint from Trawsfynydd to Bala, and needed a reliable crossing at this point over the rocky bed of Afon Taihirion. Other routes were used by drovers who collected cattle and sheep from Ynys Môn and Llŷn and moved these animals through the mountains to England where they were sold in the markets of the big cities.

The sight of these slow-moving columns of animals controlled by drovers riding their sturdy Welsh ponies must have been striking. The column would take twenty minutes to pass and might stretch for over half a mile. The drover was a cattle dealer who in the 18th century sometimes became rich and influential. They carried news of important events, such as the defeat of Napoloen at Waterloo, and spread new ideas about farming, such as the use of turnips as a winter feed for livestock. They kept detailed accounts and also acted as bankers for farmers who trusted them with their money.

Many of the roads used by the drovers have been lost or become minor roads that are now used only to link hill farms. They tended to avoid main roads to save paying tolls, and needed wide grass verges for grazing as the animals moved on the hoof at about two miles an hour.

In open country, where farmers wanted the drovers to stay overnight, they planted three Scots pines that were visible over great distances as a welcome sign to the weary herdsmen. Some farms in out of the way places became inns and provided adjoining pasture for the cattle and sheep.

An example of an old drovers' road can be traced on the Ordnance Survey map from Penmachno to Ysbyty Ifan, crossing Afon Rhydyrhalen and Afon Eidda, with paved sections still clearly visible.

The cattle came up from Dyffryn Maentwrog (Vale of

Ffestiniog) to Pont yr Afon Gam and then either crossed the Migneint to Bala or to Ysbyty Ifan through wide stretches of peat bog. Except in summer, these tracks were almost impassable, since the bog comes right up to the edge of the road.

After 2 miles (3.2km) the track forked to Cwm Penmachno and a large well called Ffynnon Eidda provided water for men and their stock at this junction. It has stood for centuries though the present structure was rebuilt as recently as 1846. Its inscription reads appropriately 'Ffynnon Eidda yf a bydd ddiolchgar' (drink and be thankful).

The cattle moved to Pentrefoelas, which was an important place for collecting animals and then on to the shoeing station at Cerrigydrudion. The animals (cattle mostly, but sheep, pigs and even geese were moved in this way) then moved eastwards to Rhuthun where there was a Drovers' Arms just north of the town. A few miles to the south-east, the small village of Graig Fechan also had its inn, called the Three Pigeons, which had to be enlarged in the 18th century to accommodate the increased numbers of drovers using this route to England.

The old bridges, the roadside wells, paved upland tracks and ruined inns recall this period of droving cattle which ended around 1850-1870 with the coming of the age of railways.

In 'Wild Wales' (1862) George Borrow refers to this bridge at Tai Hirion. He was on his way across the Migneint to Bala. On his way he

> 'passed over moors, black and barren, along a dusty road till I came to a valley; I was now almost choked with dust and thirst, and longed for nothing in the world so much as for water; suddenly I heard its blessed sound, and perceived a rivulet on my left hand. It was crossed by two bridges, one immensely old and terribly dilapidated, the other old enough, but in better repair – went and drank under the oldest bridge of the two. The water tasted of the peat of the moors, nevertheless I drank greedily of it, for one must not be over-delicate upon the moors.
>
> Refreshed with my draught, I proceed briskly on my way,

and in a little time saw a range of white buildings, diverging from the road on the right hand, the gable of the first abutting upon it. A kind of farmyard was before them. A respectable-looking woman was standing in the yard. I went up to her and inquired the name of the place.

'These houses, sir', said she, 'are called Tai Hirion Mignaint. Look over that door and you will see. T.H., which letters stand for Tai Hirion, Mignaint is the name of the place where they stand.'

I looked, and upon a stone which formed the lintel of the middlemost door I read T.H. 1630.

The words Tai Hirion, it will be as well as to say, signify the long houses.

I looked long and steadfastly at the inscription, my mind full of thoughts of the past.'

Tai Hirion was occupied during the summer months by a shepherd and his family until the early 1940's. By the late 1970's it was a ruin and was demolished. A heap of stones remains to mark the position of this lonely moorland farm.

41. CAE COCH
CAE COCH COTTAGE (GR 733715)

Old Cottage – Cae Coch above Ro-wen

Cae Coch is a single-storey, white-washed cottage that stands on the Roman road from Canovium (Caerhun) to Segontium (Caernarfon), near its highest point over Bwlch y Ddeufaen. The cottage is one of the latest in a succession of monuments dating back to 3,500BC which survive in abundance in the area. The earliest evidence is the Neolithic chambered-tomb at Maen-y-Bardd east of Cae Coch and, in the next field, the astonishing Ffon-y-Cawr, which is an early prehistoric Standing Stone that leans at an amazing angle. On the western side of Cae Coch, near the summit of the pass, are the two Bronze Age Stones that give the pass its name, for Bwlch y Ddeufaen means 'the pass of the two stones'. The Iron Age is well represented by the two hill-top camps with their ditches and banks at Pen-y-gaer and Caer Bach. In this historical 'theme park' is the Roman road that runs only a few yards in front of Cae Coch and lies in a sunken hollow between two marked banks. It strikes in a straight line, broken only by a 'modern' field wall, towards the head of the pass. Settlement continued into the medieval period, as shown by the field walls, but it was not until the 18th and 19th centuries that the value of the pass was rediscovered by the Drovers using this short-cut for driving their cattle and sheep from Ynys Môn to England.

It is probable that Cae Coch originated as

Old Cottage – Crogloft at Cae Coch

a tŷ unnos (see 115) but, since no legal documents were issued, it is difficult to establish the exact history of any of the tai unnos. No rights of ownership existed on un-enclosed moorland so it attracted the attention of landless men, especially in the period 1780 to 1820. One strong clue to the origin of these cottages on the moors is the word 'newydd' (new) which was sometimes adopted as the name of the cottage. The field at the back of Cae Coch is called 'cae newydd', which could be a distinguishing clue to its origin. However, the first recorded name for Cae Coch was 'Waen Penny' which is shown as a hovel on early maps of the 19th century, and is a clear indication that it was used by Drovers who drove cattle from Ynys Môn across Traeth Lafan to

Aber and then up the valley to Bwlch y Ddeufaen. The old cottage was a useful overnight stop for the Drovers, where they could sleep while their animals grazed. The field below the cottage still retains the name 'Waen Penny' and is shown on the Tithe Map of 1840. It shows that this is where the Drovers grazed their animals and paid a half-penny a head for each beast.

About 1830 the Drovers ceased to use this route because Thomas Telford had built Pont y Borth (Menai Bridge) and the Drovers took the easier route along the coast or through Nant Ffrancon to Dyffryn Conwy. Bwlch y Ddeufaen continued to be used for overland travel, but failed to become a Turnpike Trust road. The land in Caerhun parish was mainly enclosed in 1859 and the old cottage of Waen Penny was re-built in stone with two rooms and a crog-loft. The former position of the hearth and the stone-walled path to the old cottage were retained. A slate roof and a bread oven were built and slate slabs replaced the previous clay floor. A ladder gave access to the loft, which was used as a bedroom. It was used to house a farm labourer and his family. In the 1861 Census the labourer was William Thomas but his sons, like those of his neighbours, worked in the granite quarry at Penmaenmawr. It's main advantage over the neighbouring fifteen cottages, which all relied on wells, was an unfailing supply of pure drinking water behind the cottage. It is released from a large peat bog and never dried up, even in the famous drought of 1976.

The owner gave his new abode a new name to befit its higher status as a stone-built cottage, and Cae Coch it has been ever since. The only concession to the Drovers was the field name 'Waen Penny'. The reason for the new name of 'Cae Coch' (red field) remained a mystery until 1989. The field around the cottage had been used for sheep grazing and hay, and this consequently caused the reddish-brown sorrel that had previously flourished here to fail. The mystery was solved when the owner had to dig up the field for electricity cables. In the following June, after a period without grazing, the sour-tasting but distinctly red sorrel flourished again.

The cottage retained the original hearth at its western end and the bread oven was set in the wall diagonally opposite the main fireplace. The early owners used furze, which grew abundantly and gave an intense heat. The ashes were removed, the bread put in and the door closed and sealed tightly with freshly dug clay. The oven also provided heating, thus explaining why they were placed within the house rather than in outbuildings. The other main feature was the crog-loft which 'hung' over the main room. Access to it was gained by a ladder.

Many of these farmsteads and cottages were built in the 1850's when Caerhun common was enclosed to improve farming practices. Enclosure walls were built and these are a major feature of the present landscape. Most of these 'tyddyns' created by the Enclosure awards were 'long houses' which incorporated a cowshed, a dairy and a pig sty. But Cae Coch differed from this pattern for it was just a two-roomed cottage with a crog-loft. It was much later that the owner built a separate cow byre and pig sty and it was not until 1910 that he added a hay-barn. In more recent times a bathroom was added, electricity was connected and the hay-barn became extra accommodation.

Unlike the other farmsteads it has survived because of its unfailing clean water supply and its position adjacent to the only metal-surfaced road up to the cattle-grid at the end of the road up to Bwlch y Ddeufaen.

42. POWER OF THE WATER MILLS
WATER MILLS – 18th CENTURY

Mills for grinding corn in Dyffryn Conwy date back to medieval times. In the reign of Edward I (1284), two mills are mentioned at Conwy itself, one by the castle. The people in Conwy had to use the town mills on Afon Gyffin, which flows into the estuary near the castle. There were strict rules governing the work of the millers, who had to 'grind corn for every person as their corn comes, not to be absent in time of grinding'. The miller also had to see that 'every sack be truly filled without fraud'.

As time passed, the rich water-power resources of Afon Conwy led to the growth of mills on the main stream and on other streams flowing into Afon Conwy. By the end of the 18th century, the valley had more than its fair share of water-driven mills. An exact record of the location of these mills is shown on a map of north Wales drawn in 1797 by John Evans, who used a small-wheel symbol to show every working mill. This map is an accurate and reliable document showing the villages, churches, large country houses, roads and tracks. Travellers placed their complete trust in the accuracy of this map.

The mills were situated on steep rivers, near villages or adjacent to a main road in days when transport of corn to the mill was a problem. In some favoured spots, Evans's map showed two mills close together, such as a mill below Eglwysbach and one above the village on the same stream.

Edward Pugh visited Caerhun Hall and then went on to a 'nearby overshot mill'. He then went on a little further to Rowen, where a 'raging torrent had moved many rocks and boulders, tore up a meadow and carried with it a mill and several houses. The river has changed course since this flood.'

Every stream flowing off the coastal hills had its own mill, at Penrhyn, Rhos, Colwyn and Llanddulas, all of which are shown on Evans's map. In the upper regions of the valley there were corn mills at Trefriw, Penmachno, Pentrefoelas and

Nant Mill near Betws Garmon

Dolwyddelan. Mills are also recorded on the map at Dwygyfylchi and at Llanrwst.

Further evidence about these old mills can be seen in written accounts, such as that of Walter Bingley, who in 1798 'stopped at a fulling mill near a bridge, Pont y Pandy. Here a waterfall called Rhaeadr y Graig Lwyd is not very lofty and a rude wooden aqueduct carries water to an old overshot mill overgrown with moss and grass.'

This refers to the mill at Pont y Pandy near Penmachno, which is near a still flourishing woollen mill. Pandy is the Welsh word for a fulling mill. Cottagers would spin wool at home on a spinning wheel although the more well-to-do farmers would have a hand-weaving loom, and the rough cloth would need to be smoothed. They would therefore take the rough cloth to be moistened and beaten under fulling hammers at the mill, which would matt the fibres and give a smooth finish to the cloth.

These fulling mills were common in late 18th century Wales

and the name 'pandy' is a very common place-name. The fulling mill at Penmachno was originally part of a corn-grinding mill because in 1811 a local newspaper advertised the mill as 'a corn-grist mill with three pairs of grinding stones and a woollen factory adjoining'.

Apart from the word 'pandy', the word 'melin' also shows the sites of these early mills. The typical mill of this period was a stone building on the sides of a narrow rocky gorge with a fast-flowing stream giving abundant water in all seasons.

A wooden leet or trough would carry the water from a weir to an overshot wheel which turned the grinding stones or fulling hammers. They were in attractive spots and there are Romantic engravings in many of the contemporary travel books.

Of the many mills dating back to 1797 and shown on Evans' map, four still survive as working mills at Trefriw, Felin Isaf in Glan Conwy, Pentrefoelas and Pont y Pandy in Penmachno. All of these mills are open to visitors and are a splendid legacy of an early industrial age.

43. FORGOTTEN VILLAGE OF STONE MEN
ARENNIG – ABANDONED QUARRY VILLAGE (GR 833393)

Remains of Arennig Village and abandoned Granite Quarry

In 1908 a granite quarry was opened at the foot of the towering Arennig Fawr on the desolate Migneint moors. For over half a century it supplied roadstone, chippings for railway tracks, and cubic setts for paving. The Bala-Ffestiniog railway provided the essential link, bringing in quarrymen on the early train, taking children and shoppers to Bala, and bringing the postman with mail and bread. Apart from the station master and two signalmen, all the men worked in the quarry and Arennig village grew up along the single road below the quarry, but no longer appears on the map.

Life was hard and basic for, apart from milk from the farm, eggs and homegrown potatoes, the villagers depended on a weekly visit to Bala or Ffestiniog for their food supplies. Water flowed abundantly off Arennig mountain and was tapped in springs and spouts near the houses. The small cottages were lit by candles and oil-lamps.

In preparation for hard winters they filled large earthenware tubs with salted butter, kept a sack of flour and some yeast and kept a hod of potatoes grown during the summer in one or two rows near the house. Peat that was dug in summer from the floor of Cwm Tryweryn, or from flat bogs on the slopes of Arennig, was dried and stored near the house. They had to be prepared for the days or weeks when snow closed the roads, and even the railway cuttings were sometimes completely blocked.

In the early years, a loft above the stable of the farm was used as a chapel, but this was later replaced by a zinc-coated steel chapel which is still standing. Most of the villagers however preferred to walk three miles to the old stone chapel at Capel Celyn, where eisteddfodau and concerts were held. Children also had to walk this distance to Capel Celyn village school, where a clothes drying room was often used.

The chief pleasure was fishing in the well-stocked Afon Tryweryn and the nearby mountain streams. The mountain pools were rich in black trout, which tasted sweeter than the brown trout of Afon Tryweryn. In the 1920s and 1930s the village boasted a large population, with between thirty and forty children of secondary school age catching the school train to Bala. Today only two houses remain of the village and its buildings have gone. It is now only of interest to the industrial archaeologist.

Ironically, one of the buildings still standing is the powder magazine, a solid stone building near the river. In the old days it was out of bounds except to the rock man (creigiwr) in charge of blasting. The zinc chapel still stands, but all the houses except two have disappeared. The railway track can be traced only where it runs through a cutting or stands on an embankment; and there is no trace of the railway station. A few ruined walls mark the site of former buildings and the foundations of the bridge from the quarry to the crusher on the railway survive.

Tryweryn Halt – disused railway track, coach and station house.

The source of the failure of the village and quarry dates from the drowning of Cwm Tryweryn below the waterfalls in 1965 to create Llyn Celyn, so that the citizens of Liverpool could enjoy good, clean, cheap water. The city council maintained throughout that no more than a handful of smallholders would suffer from the drowning of this valley. What made the dispute so bitter was that a totally Welsh community was, if not exactly disappearing under the doubtlessly useful waters, then being dispersed to seek a living and to join a new community elsewhere. In the process, the $3^1/_2$ miles (5.5km) of railway track that was also submerged meant that the Bala-Ffestiniog railway had to close. The numerous villagers of Arennig had depended on the railway, for road transport of granite was expensive. The people slowly moved away thus creating difficulty in getting enough labour for the quarry. Most of the houses and quarry buildings were demolished. All that remains of a once-flourishing industry are the scarred hillside with its galleries.

44. CIDER STOP ON A ROCKY RIDE NORTH
TURNPIKE TRUST ROAD (GR 721580)

Toll House at Capel Curig

Until 1791 there was no road from Nant Ffrancon to Capel Curig, and it was one of the most isolated spots in north Wales. There were paths or tracks up Nant Ffrancon to Llyn Ogwen, but Thomas Pennant described the track there as 'the most dreadful horse path in Wales, worked in the rudest manner in steps for a great length.'

This situation changed in 1791-2 when Lord Penrhyn, who was then taking over and opening up the slate quarries at Bethesda, made a road up the western side of Nant Ffrancon and continued it on to Capel Curig. His intention was to encourage travellers to his newly built Capel Cerrig Inn which later became the Royal Hotel, and today is the mountaineering centre of Plas-y-Brenin.

The new road was suitable for carriages and many visitors

were brought to the Inn from Ireland – mainly government officials and military officers. Visitors also came to Eryri because Europe was out of bounds due to the Napoleonic Wars.

By 1798, many quide books were being published and a flood of visitors needed overnight accommodation. The inn was comfortable and Griffith, the inn-keeper, was much praised by visitors for his hospitality. Carriages brought travellers and horses were changed for a continuation of the journey to the next stop at Cernioge near Pentrefoelas.

The inn register records some of the news of the visitors, such as the dangers of travelling in darkness without a guide. One visitor records that 'the beer and cider is now most excellent. How long it may continue, he (Griffith) knows not. The bottles break and the liquor finds various ways to escape daily. The sooner it is called for the better. It will not keep.' The man would probably go to Ibiza if he were still around today.

The new road from Nant Ffrancon ran along the foot of Tryfan passing the farmhouse at Gwern y Gof, and then through boggy, uneven ground along the western side of Afon Llugwy. This is now a fine 'green road' which is shown as a footpath on the map. In the last decade of the 18th century, it was capable of carrying a horse and coach bringing visitors to Capel Curig. But in winter, frost, snow and rain would have often made it impassable. The farmers who use the road today complain of its boggy, uneven and rock-strewn surface.

It was ten years before the road to Betws-y-coed and on to Pentrefoelas was constructed. The Capel Curig Turnpike Trust was formed by Act of Parliament in 1802. The trust borrowed money and used it to build a road from Capel Curig over Pont Cyfyng to Betws-y-coed. It then followed the sides of what became known as the Fairy Glen to Pentrefoelas.

This toll-operated road was short-lived because it only lasted until 1819 when the Trust was wound up and the road was re-built by Telford. The Trust collected tolls to pay for the interest on the loan to construct the road and for its upkeep. Toll-houses were built at Capel Curig (Ty'n Lôn), Betws-y-coed and Hendre

Isaf. These gates were working by 1803 and the toll-keepers were paid 35p a week. In 1806, the gates were let annually for a rent of £250. Tolls charged were 8p for a horse and coach, $1^1/_2$p for a horse; cattle, sheep and pigs also had to be paid for and double tolls were payable on Sundays.

There were some exemptions, notably for the farmers who could take their animals to market at Llanrwst. People who took a short-cut to avoid passing the toll-gate were fined and no-one was allowed to drag timber or stone along the road.

The Trustees set up milestones measured from the nearest towns. These improvements were of great value in opening up the area and from September 8, 1808 the road was deemed good enough for the Shrewsbury-Holyhead mail-coach from Pentrefoelas to go through Capel Curig, instead of using the old road through Nebo and Llanrwst.

Books of the period show prints of four horses and a coach bowling along at speeds of 8-10 mph. This road survives as a footpath or a narrow country lane with tollhouses as the most striking reminder. These can be identified by windows that jut out so that the toll-keeper could see along the road in both directions. A fine specimen is Ty'n Lôn, Capel Curig – the tollhouse with probably the finest view in Britain.

45. INN FIT FOR A QUEEN TESTED DUKE'S NERVE
CERNIOGE – COACHING INN (GR 905505)

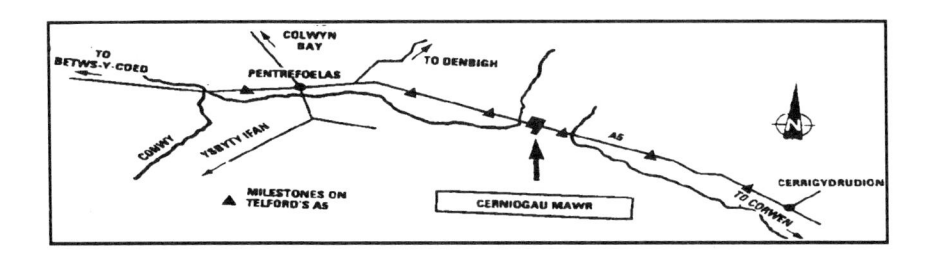

After trudging from Conwy during a walking holiday in August, 1797, the Revd Warner arrived at the Prince Llywelyn Inn near Pentrefoelas, on a long desolate section of the coach road. He described how he arrived at 'this place at 8 o'clock, a solitary inn in the midst of a desert, chiefly intended for coaches which run this road. The larder has nothing but a leg of mutton, which we ordered to be roasted, although we doubt whether a very keen appetite produced by a

An old milestone near Maentwrog

The Old Coach Road near Betws-y-coed

fasting walk of 26 miles (42km) will render it eatable'.

The inn was at Cerniogau or Cerniogau Mawr, a name that can be traced back to the Middle Ages when it appears in the Charter of Aberconwy Abbey as part of their sheep-grazing pasture belonging to the Abbot. It later became the residence of a local noble family, and is shown on John Evans' map of 1797. But its greatest fame dates from 1808 when it became a posting inn where stagecoaches stopped on their journey from London to Holyhead. Apart from the Nant Ffrancon, this was the highest point on the route.

The innkeeper had stables for sixty-nine horses so there was an assured supply of fresh horse power to enable stagecoaches to keep to their scheduled 10mph (16km/p/h). The inn had a good reputation for feeding and caring for the horses, which is shown by a story told by the Duke of Wellington in the House of Commons. He claimed that he preferred the road to Holyhead via Cerniogau to the coast route and always found the best team at Cerniogau. On one occasion however, the

A Toll Gate formerly on Telford's A5, now a farm gate near Pentrefoelas

horses trotted so well down the rather steep slope from Pentrefoelas to Betws-y-coed that at Conwy Falls the duke, who was noted for his iron nerve, cried out: 'For God's sake, do take time'.

It was in the period just after Telford's A5 had been opened (1826), that Cerniogau reached its greatest importance for stagecoaches. Because of road improvements the Holyhead mailcoach had, over the years, reduced the journey time from London to Holyhead from 38 hours in 1817, to 26 hours 55 minutes in 1836. The Mail left London at 8pm and reached Corwen at 4pm the following day. The coach stopped at Cerniogau for a change of horses at 5.39 pm, and arrived at Holyhead at 10.55 pm. This was the fastest time ever achieved over the 260 mile (418km) by the Irish mail.

Queen Victoria visited the Prince Llywelyn some five years before her accession to the throne, when the menu had improved somewhat, and a brass tablet over the fireplace in the sitting room recalled the visit with the inscription: 'Queen

Victoria had tea in this room on her journey from Wynnstay to Beaumaris in the summer of 1832'.

In 1839, the inn's licence was transferred to the Foelas Arms at Pentrefoelas, which was in a better position and, in 1856, a guide recorded that Cerniogau Mawr had been converted into a farmhouse. Its importance is shown by the fact that references appear in most of the travel books of the time, and its name appears on milestones set up by Telford on the A5. An even earlier milestone standing on the bridge at Maentwrog records distances to London (220), Dolgellau (18), Bala (22) and Cerniogau (20).

Today Cerniogau Mawr is a farm on both sides of the A5 about $2^1/_2$ miles (4km) east of Pentrefoelas.

46. THE STAGE-COACH AT TY'N Y COED
STAGE COACH AT TY'N Y COED (GR 734572)

The black and yellow stage-coach on the A5 outside the Ty'n y Coed Hotel, Capel Curig is a reminder of the golden age of coach travel (1820-40) when, for the first time in history, travel became more easy and secure. A coachman handling four horses could maintain 11mph (18km/p/h) on this section of Telford's newly-built road. He was charged with supervising the luggage on the roof of the coach and keeping to the number of passengers as allowed by regulations.

A milestone on Telford's A5 near Betws-y-coed

Inside the glass-windowed compartment on the hard wooden seats the four passengers paid twice the fare of those on the outside. Some people preferred the box-seat next to the coachman where they could observe the road, watch the coachman's skills, or perhaps even persuade him to hand over the reins for a short spell. This was strictly illegal and often timid passengers or roadside informers would report such incidents to the coach owners. Behind the coachman there was room for three more passengers

Stage Coach near Capel Curig

and another four at the back. This was the most uncomfortable part of the coach; they were jolted by the motion of the coach and lurched sideways on a sharp bend. They also had to face the weather – frost and snow in winter, dust and heat in summer. Only the hardiest traveller could endure riding outside as the coach travelled through the night. The coach stopped every ten miles to change horses and in usually took less than three minutes to harness a fresh team. To the mail coach every minute counted as it kept to a strict timetable. Every other coach or road-user had to give way, and the mail-coach was exempt from the tolls that delayed other coaches. As the toll-gate came into sight the guard would blow his horn and the toll-keeper would rush out of the toll-house to open the gates. The guards threw the mail-bags into the arms of the waiting post-masters in the wayside villages without stopping the coach.

By 1836 the Irish mail left London at 8.00 p.m. and travelled through the night reaching Birmingham the following morning at 7.00 a.m. It reached Corwen in the afternoon at 4.00 p.m. and they changed horses at Cernioge at 5.39p.m. The coach then crossed the Waterloo Bridge at Betws-y-coed and was passing the Ty'n Lôn toll-house at Capel Curig at 7.02 p.m. before its climb to Llyn Ogwen and its descent of Nant Ffrancon and on to Pont y Borth (Menai Bridge). The weary travellers reached Holyhead at 10.55 p.m. and the guard discharged his mail, including letters for Ireland, as his final duty.

From about 1840 the great days of the stage-coach were over, for the railways gave faster, cheaper transport. They could also of course take larger numbers of people, many of whom had never travelled before. With trains reaching speeds of 30 mph (48km/p/h), 'everything is near, everything is immediate – time, distance and delay are abolished' became the boast of 1842. The rattle of the stage-coach wheels, the resounding hooves of the horses and the guard's horn summoning the toll-keeper to open the gates had become nothing more than a distant memory by the 1880's. The stage-coach at Ty'n y Coed, the toll-houses, a few of Telfords rectangular heavy wrought-iron gates and the redundant milestones are however reminders of transport in the early 19th century.

47. FEARFUL TREK OVER A RIVER'S SANDTRAP
CROSSING THE CONWY ESTUARY (GR 790780)

When the Napoleonic Wars closed the Continent to British travellers towards the end of the 18th century, it became fashionable to tour Wales, on foot, on horseback or by coach and horses, in search of the elusive picturesque. Among such visitors was the Revd Warner of Bath who, in 1797 and 1798 completed two walks around Wales, keeping mainly to the coast and the border with England. His book records the day-to-day account of his journeys with detailed information on distances walked, the weather, the food, conversations with local people, and the Inns where he stayed.

On the 28th August, 1797, he commented on the view of Conwy Castle as 'the most sublime ruin in the Kingdom; its magnificent castle'. Having walked all day from Caernarfon, he reached Conwy at 8 p.m. and stayed at The Bull's Head where, despite being a pedestrian, he received a great welcome from the inn-keeper who said he was used to mountain walkers.

The two girl-waitresses were cheerful, friendly and as beautiful as Turkish dancers. After a good meal, the guests were entertained by the renowned blind harpist, Mr Jones, who played the ancient triple-stringed Welsh harp. The following morning the Revd Warner walked around Conwy and visited 'the stupendous castle as far as the rising tide would allow us round its outward walls to see a ruined tower. It forms a scene of devastation. The rock on which it was built having been excavated for the sake of its stone, the lower part of the tower gave way and tumbled in mighty fragments to the shore beneath leaving the upper half hanging in the air, and a nodding ruin on all who venture to approach it.'

He was impressed with the fine house of Plas mawr which was a vast pile, decorated within and without in fantastic fashion with ornaments of stone and plaster consisting of coats of arms, scrutcheons, nests, birds and beasts. Conwy must have

Conwy ferry

made a good impression on the Revd Warner because, in the following August, he was back having crossed Afon Conwy from Deganwy.

On this journey he had walked 29 miles (46km) from Caerwys past St Asaph and Rhuddlan Castle. He stopped for lunch at 'the little bathing town of Abergele' where he had excellent London ale, Shropshire cheese and bread. It was evening when he reached the passage-house or ferry opposite Conwy. The tide was out and they had to face a three-quarter mile walk across the sands to where the ferry boat was waiting.

Warner was worried about the wisdom of crossing so late in the evening and there was no guide available.

The man at the ferry-house dismissed Warner's fears with a sarcastic grin, that if they were quick, they should overtake a group who would act as guides and protectors. These guides turned out to be three old women who were crossing the river to Conwy to sell butter and eggs. Warner followed them but failed to catch them up; 'they crossed the brook in the sands by wading through it after pulling off their stockings and shoes and tucking up their petticoats to their middle'. Warner remained doubtful about crossing because the sands gave way under their feet, the tide was coming in and it was getting dark. They were, however, favoured by moonlight and at last reached the waiting ferry-boat and crossed to the quay at Conwy. He was happy to have reached the 'old quarters' at the Bull's Head and was again given a good supper and the best hospitality.

48. TELL-TALES FROM A HORSE-POWER ERA
STABLE LOFTS – FRONGOCH (GR 903394)

Loft above the Stables, Frongoch Farm near Bala

Many north Wales farms have a building with an outside staircase of stone steps that lead to a large under-roof loft. A door, and perhaps a porch set in the slated roof can sometimes be seen, as well as a kennel set in the base of the stairs. From about 1870 sheep dogs became common on farms in North Wales and also acted as guard dogs to protect vital stores in the granary. The wooden-floored loft was used as a granary at a time when the farm depended totally on horses, and large quantities of oats had to be stored for winter feed. On farms near Cerrigydrudion, at least 30 acres (13 hectares) were needed to grow oats to feed the horses.

An eyewitness remembers as a very small boy at Hendre Isaf, Llangernyw, the granary was reached via a wooden staircase inside the building. On the left at the top of the staircase was the granary and on the right the stable loft – this being used for fodder only and not for sleeping. Beneath the granary various agricultural implements were stored.

One year in the early 1920s when the harvest had been unusually good, the granary was piled high with grain after threshing day.

During the night the wooden floor gave way and the grain cascaded into the storage space below. A highly polished horse-drawn trap and an American self-delivery reaper were two of the many implements almost buried by the grain. One of the larger bedrooms in the house was emptied of furniture and used for grain storage until the floor was renewed.

As regards the stable lofts, he slept in one at Gloddaeth, Llanelian for twelve months from 1938-39. Although there was no fireplace he never remembers being cold during the winter nights. Many more farm workers in that area slept in outside lofts.

This arrangement may have been convenient for the farmer but it was also convenient for the worker – there being no check on times of return from their various evening activities.

Below the loft the building housed the essential carts and these cartsheds appear in the list of goods for sale at farm auctions. Such was the case at Hafod-y-garreg near Pentrefoelas, which was sold in 1891 and two carts are listed in the sale inventory. On Hafod-y-maidd farm near Cerrigydrudion, the three cart sheds survive in excellent condition, as well as the second-storey granary above with its tell-tale windows.

The granary sometimes had latticed windows to give good ventilation to keep the grain dry. Sometimes shutters were used to keep out wind and rain, but other problems were inquisitive and hungry birds. The walls were limewashed or plastered and the floors kept in good repair to prevent rats and mice from getting at the grain.

The earliest known dated granary is on a farm at Glan Conwy, where the date 1795 can be seen on a wooden rafter. Most of the early dates are between 1816-20 which suggests that this was the main period when the building of granaries became common. Some granaries were also erected above the stables.

The oats and hay could then be dropped into the feeding racks below through a trap door or hole.

The loft was called in Welsh, 'llofft y stabl' which more or less explains itself. Because they were clean, dry and well ventilated they also found a use as extra bedrooms on many farms. In the 19th century and up to the 1940s, farms relied on many farm workers, before mechanisation came to replace them. The young unmarried male workers had to live on the farm and, to accommodate them, the farmer often partitioned the loft and put in a fireplace and beds. Apart from the noise of the mice scurrying around the wainscots of the granary next door, it was said to be easy to sleep there on a cold night. The warmth from the horses below, the insulation of the grain next door and the smouldering embers of the fire provided a cosy sort of comfort.

This practice of sleeping in the stable lofts survived in the remotest parts of the Llŷn Peninsula until after the Second World War. But on Fron Goch farm near Bala, I was told that two farm workers slept in the loft until 1932. The farmers were happy with this custom because the horses could be looked after and attended to in an emergency during the long winter nights.

The horses remained important until the 1930's when tractors eventually came to replace them. The stables were then put to other uses such as for oil storage, tractor sheds and garages. Also, the need for extra workers outside of the family gradually died out on the smaller farms so that the stable loft was no longer needed as a dormitory.

The buildings, however, with their outside staircases still survive on many farms, and are part of our rural heritage.

49. SPRINGS OF HEALING IN A RED FIELD
TREFRIW SPA (GR 778653)

Old Bath-House at Trefriw Spa

The Celts knew about and valued mineral springs. Their most notable one was the site of the hot springs at Bath, dedicated to the local deity, Sulis. The Romans took over the shrine and developed a temple and baths in their new settlement, calling it Aquae Sulis (Bath).

In Dyffryn Conwy, the best known mineral spring lies one mile north of Trefriw, and may have also been known to the Romans, for it was near their road from Canovium (Caerhun) to the small fort at Bryn Gefeiliau near Tŷ Hyll. The river meadows of Afon Conwy at Trefriw Spa rise to a steep slope, where a unique deposit of iron pyrites (fool's gold) has been worked for sulphur. The six-foot thick vein of iron and sulphur shows up as a layer of minute brass-coloured cubes. The rainwater falling on the mountain percolates through the ore-body and absorbs the iron sulphides in solution. It then flows out at the foot of the slope as a chalybeate spring. Trefriw Spa is notable because of the thickness and purity of the chalybeate deposit in the hills, and for the volume and quality of the mineral-rich water issuing out as a spring.

The exact spot is called Cae Coch, and was known to be locally famous for its water as far back as 1756. The springs were subsequently covered by a landslide, and were not rediscovered until 1833.

Today the springs can still be seen and are protected behind a door that opens into a small chamber with three caves running underground into the mountain. The water temperature is always 32°F and the level of the water is constant whatever the season or amount of rainfall. The warmth of the caves encourages evaporation of soluble minerals, and they have formed a dense forest of multi-coloured stalactites.

Two of the caves are floodlit to expose these stalactites, which are reflected in the crystal-clear waters of the subterranean pools. The third cave is sealed so that the pure water can be pumped out to the bottling room, without any contact with the air.

The caves were originally linked by pipe to a two-roomed bath-house built a few feet below the caves. Huge blocks of stone were used and the drystone walls are a remarkable feature of this style of 'cyclopean' architecture. The large, slate-lined bath and the spring-fed pipes hint at the bathing methods used when this building was in use.

The development of the Spa reached its fullest development in Victorian days when road, rail and even a paddle-steamer brought large numbers of people to Trefriw. There were also many medical reports recommending the therapeutic use of the waters at Trefriw. The new building in 1874 housed a main hall that was used for social purposes and modern baths were installed in an adjoining wing.

The water was brought to the pump room by pipe to prevent air contact and there was never any shortage, even in a severe drought. Rheumatic diseases, anaemia, depression, blood and nerve conditions were treated. The Spa continued to be important until the 1930s and in The Lancet in 1930 a medical authority claimed that 'the waters of Trefriw stood at the head of all chalybeate waters of Europe'.

Unlike most chalybeate waters, the Trefriw water travels well and was bottled and sent to all parts of Britain and abroad. Tickets to the baths were issued as late as 1937 and the order books for bottled water continued up to 1959. These can be seen in the Spa today.

There are many memories and souvenirs of the Spa still surviving in the area. There are people who remember the Oxford vans being loaded up daily with bottled water. There are collections of stamps and postcards that were posted to Trefriw from all parts of the world.

The pump room and bath house were restored in 1972. Through a guided tour of the underground caves and the cyclopean bath house, today's visitors can get a fascinating insight into the past.

50. CHALYBEATE WELL AT YSBYTY IFAN
(GR846485)

The church at Ysbyty Ifan

Towards the end of the 19th Century the local people in Ysbyty Ifan knew about the chalybeate well on a small stream southeast of the village. As at Trefriw the mineral water filling the well was impregnated with native carbonate of iron which occurs in the rocks crossing the river further up stream. They would have recognized the rust - coloured water in the well and realized its beneficial effects as well, according to local opinion, its curative effects on warts. There appears to be no documentary sources about the history of the well apart from its existence shown on The First Edition of the Ordnance Survey Map in the 1880's. It is shown as a 'well' just on the edge of Tŷ Nant farm. The only evidence now is in the collective memory of the oldest residents who have lived in the village all their lives and as young people recall a wooden structure which had been built to enclose the well. Nothing exists today but one man born in 1920 who worked as a young man on Tŷ Nant Farm recalls the extreme coldness of the water and how he drank lots of it for its medicinal quality. The local children with warts on their hands were told to go there and hold their hands under the water for as long as they could bear it and then to plaster the rust-coloured sediment found at the bottom of the ditch on the warts. This was supposed to be a certain cure.

The well was enclosed by a wooden hut at the end of the 19th century and by 1916 was weather beaten and in need of repair. It had a door and wooden planks around the inside walls which served as seats. The buildings was about sixteen feet long by ten feet wide. Another witness says that it was still standing in the early 1920's but by about 1927-8 it had been demolished. During the 1920's many villagers used the well as a source of drinking water and used quart milk cans which had a lid and fairly wide flat handle to carry it back home. It is not certain why it was demolished but its popularity was in decline. Its hey-day was in the first decade of the 20th century which may have coincided with the Methodist Revival of 1905; a nearby Methodist chapel may support this view. It remained a popular meeting place especially for young people who gathered there for impromptu singing of hymns on summer evenings. This was similar to the hymn singing in the village where farm servants and others gathered by the shop or smithy, and continued late into the night.

There is therefore no record of who built the shed over the Tŷ Nant chalybeate well in the first place. Some local person or even the parish council who thought it had some medical value to the community. The two parishes then had a population of a thousand at the end of the 19th century. Each parish was separated by Afon Conwy which runs through the village and it also formed the boundary between Caernarfonshire and Denbighshire. On the Caernarfonshire side the Penrhyn Arms

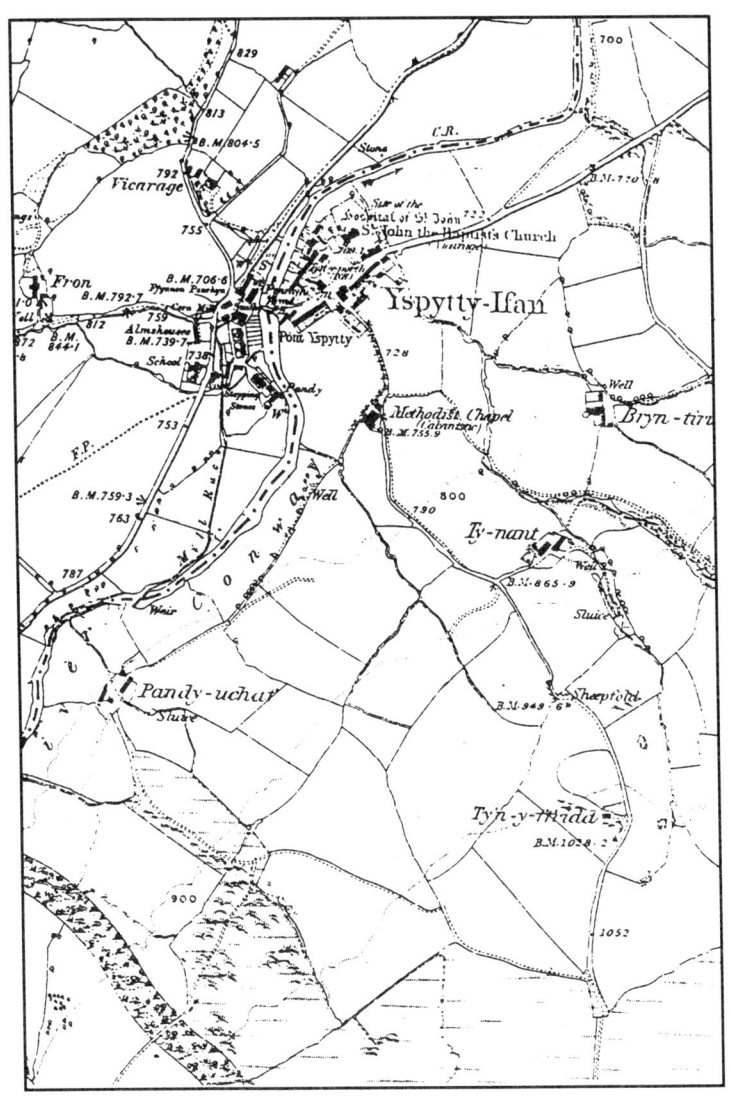

Ysbyty Ifan

was an important pub with its closing time at 10 pm. On the Denbighshire side the Ty'n-y-Porth pub closed at 9 pm. Both were farms as well as pubs but both closed as the population declined and remain as private houses today.

ACKNOWLEDGMENTS

The author wishes to thank the copyright holders who have kindly permitted the reproduction of photographs as follows:
The Moel Siabod Shield (p.34) – British Museum
Hadrianic Milestone (p.51) – British Museum
Constantinian Milestone (p.51) – National Library of Wales
Cruck Barn (p.109) – St Fagan's Museum Cardiff
Cruck Barn (p.110) – Ancient Monuments Society

I also wish to thank the following people who have contributed ideas, information or practical help in writing this book:
Catherine Buxton, my daughter
Mike Hill
David Hughes
John Lewis Jones
Frank Jowett
P.J. Warburton-Lee
Huw Owen
John Pierce
John Puw
Ted Thonger and, my publisher,
Myrddin ap Dafydd for his enthusiastic support and advice.

I also received unstinted help from the Record Offices at Caernarfon, Dolgellau, Ruthin and the Library Headquarters (Flintshire) at Mold. Grateful thanks also to the staff of the Royal Commission on Ancient and Historical Monuments, Aberystwyth (Wales).

WALK WITH HISTORY BOOKS
FROM
GWASG CARREG GWALCH

- **WALKS ON THE LLŶN PENINSULA**
  PART 1 – SOUTH & WEST
  – N. Burras & J. Stiff.
  ISBN 0-86381-343-7; £4.50

- **WALKS ON THE LLŶN PENINSULA**
  PART 2 – NORTH & EAST
  – N. Burras & J. Stiff.
  ISBN 0-86381-365-8; £4.50

- **WALKS IN THE SNOWDONIA MOUNTAINS**
  - Don Hinson.
  ISBN 0-86381-385-2; Revised edition; £3.75

- **WALKS IN NORTH SNOWDONIA**
  - Don Hinson.
  ISBN 0-86381-386-0; Revised edition; £3.75

- **NEW WALKS IN SNOWDONIA**
  - Don Hinson.
  ISBN 0-86381-390-9; Revised edition; £3.75

- **CIRCULAR WALKS IN NORTH PEMBROKESHIRE**
  - Paul Williams. ISBN 0-86381-420-4; £4.50

- **CIRCULAR WALKS IN SOUTH PEMBROKESHIRE**
  - Paul Willams. ISBN 0-86381-421-2; £4.50

- **FROM MOUNTAIN TOPS TO VALLEY FLOORS**
  - Salter & Worral. ISBN 0-86381-430-1; £4.50

- **CIRCULAR WALKS IN THE BRECON BEACONS NATIONAL PARK**
  ISBN 0-86381-476-X; £4.50

- **CIRCULAR WALKS ON ANGLESEY**
  Dorothy Hamilton.
  ISBN 0-86381-478-6; £4.50

- **CIRCULAR WALKS IN GOWER**
  Nick Jenkins. ISBN 0-86381-479-4; £4.50

- **CIRCULAR WALKS IN CENTRAL WALES**
  Stephen Edwards. ISBN 0-86381-480-8; £4.50

- **CIRCULAR WALKS IN GWENT**
  Richard Sale. ISBN 0-86381-477-8; £4.50

- **THE LAKES OF ERYRI**
  Geraint Roberts. ISBN 0-86381-338-0; £8.90

- **THE MOUNTAIN WALKER'S GUIDE TO WALES**
  - Colin Adams. ISBN 0-86381-154-X;
  Map, PVC cover; £6.90

- **THE BOTANISTS AND GUIDES OF SNOWDONIA**
  - Dewi Jones. ISBN 0-86381-383-6; £6.95

- **WALKS FROM LLANDUDNO**
  - Christopher Draper.
  ISBN 0-86381-559-6; £4.95

- **CIRCULAR WALKS IN MEIRIONNYDD**
  - Dorothy Hamilton. ISBN 0-86381-545-6; £4.50

- **WALKS IN AND AROUND THE BERWYN MOUNTAINS**
  - John Tranter. ISBN 0-86381-547-2; £4.50

- **CIRCULAR WALKS IN NORTH EASTERN WALES**
  - Jim Grindle. ISBN 0-86381-550-2; £4.50

- **THE NORTH WALES PATH AND TEN SELECTED WALKS**
  - Dave Salter & Dave Worrall. ISBN 0-86381-546-4; £4.50

- **LLŶN PENINSULA COASTAL WALKS**
  - Richard Quinn. ISBN 0-86381-574-X; £4.50

- **CIRCULAR WALKS IN THE BLACK MOUNTAINS**
  - Nick Jenkins. ISBN 0-86381-558-8; £4.50

- **WALKS IN THE WYE VALLEY**
  - Richard Sale. ISBN 0-86381-555-3; £4.50

- **CEREDIGION WALKS**
  Richard Sale; ISBN: 0-86381-602-9; £4.50

- **CIRCULAR WALKS IN THE VALE OF GLAMORGAN**
  Dorothy Hamilton; ISBN: 0-86381-603-7; £4.50

- **WALKS FROM COLWYN BAY**
  Chris Draper; ISBN: 0-86381-604-5; £4.95

- **A CAMBRIAN WAY**
  Richard Sale; ISBN: 0-86381-605-3; £6.90

- **CARMARTHENSHIRE COAST & GOWER CIRCULAR WALKS**
  Paul Williams; ISBN: 0-86381-607-X; £4.50

- **CIRCULAR WALKS IN THE WESTERN BEACONS**
  Nick Jenkins; ISBN: 0-86381-638-X; £4.50

- **WALKS FROM CONWY**
  - Christopher Draper
  ISBN 0-86381-695-9; £4.95

- **CIRCULAR WALKS IN THE DYFI VALLEY**
  - Dorothy Hamilton
  ISBN 0-86381-688-6; £4.50

- **OWAIN GLYNDŴR'S WAY**
  Richard Sale. ISBN 0-86381-690-8; £4.95

- **A MEIRIONNYDD COAST WALK**
  Laurence Maine. ISBN 0-86381-666-5; £5.50

- **FAMILY WALKS TO DISCOVER NORTH WALES**
  Anna & Graham Francis
  ISBN 0-86381-679-7; £4.95

Available from
GWASG CARREG GWALCH
12 Iard yr Orsaf, Llanrwst, Dyffryn Conwy,
Cymru (Wales) LL26 0EH
☎ 01492 642031
📄 01492 641502
e-bost/e-mail: books@carreg-gwalch.co.uk
lle ar y we/website: www.carreg-gwalch.co.uk

BOOKS ON SNOWDONIA FROM GWASG CARREG GWALCH

- **WALKS IN THE SNOWDONIA MOUNTAINS**
  - Don Hinson. ISBN 0-86381-385-2; £3.75

- **WALKS IN NORTH SNOWDONIA**
  - Don Hinson. ISBN 0-86381-386-0; £3.75

- **NEW WALKS IN SNOWDONIA**
  - Don Hinson. ISBN 0-86381-390-9; £3.75

- **FROM MOUNTAIN TOPS TO VALLEY FLOORS**
  - Salter & Worral. ISBN 0-86381-430-1; £4.50

- **ERYRI – THE STORY OF SNOWDONIA**
  - Michael Senior. ISBN 0-86381-549-9; £2.75

- **CAERNARFON – THE TOWN'S STORY**
  ISBN 0-86381-346-1; £1.95

- **ALL IN A DAY'S WORK**
  - David W. Earl. ISBN 0-86381-554-5; £4.95

- **SNOWDONIA, A HISTORICAL ANTHOLOGY**
  - David Kirk. ISBN 0-86381-270-8; £5.95

- **THE BOTANISTS AND GUIDES OF SNOWDONIA**
  - Dewi Jones. ISBN 0-86381-383-6; £6.95

- **THE LAKES OF ERYRI**
  - Geraint Roberts. ISBN 0-86381-338-0; £8.90

- **THE MOUNTAIN WALKER'S GUIDE TO WALES**
  - Colin Adams. ISBN 0-86381-154-X; £6.90

- **SKYWALLS - A SNOWDONIA SEQUENCE**
  Clyde Holmes. ISBN 0-86381-466-2; £5.75

- **DELVING IN DINORWIG**
  - Douglas C. Carrington. ISBN 0-86381-285-6; £7.50

- **THREE STOPS TO THE SUMMIT**
  - Rol Williams. ISBN 0-86381-433-6; £4.95

- **WINGS OF WAR OVER GWYNEDD**
  - Roy Sloan. ISBN 0-86381-189-2; £4.50

- **AIRCRAFT CRASHES IN GWYNEDD**
  - Roy Sloan. ISBN 0-86381-281-3; £5.50

Available from
GWASG CARREG GWALCH
12 Iard yr Orsaf, Llanrwst, Dyffryn Conwy,
Cymru (Wales) LL26 0EH
☎ 01492 642031
01492 641502
e-bost/e-mail: books@carreg-gwalch.co.uk
lle ar y we/website: www.carreg-gwalch.co.uk